CONDITIONING

FOR

...and then some

TOM ZUPANCIC

MASTERS PRESS

NTC/Contemporary Publishing Group

Library of Congress Cataloging-in-Publication Data

Zupancic, Tom, 1955–
    Conditioning for football / Tom Zupancic.
        p.   cm.
    ISBN 0-940279-77-0
    1. Football—Training.   I. Title.
    GV953.5.Z86   1994
    796.332'07—dc20   94-20601
                                            CIP

Cover design by Suzanne Lincoln
Photographs by Don Larson, with the exception of the Iron Man contest
photos by Jerry Clark
Diagrams by Julie Biddle
Illustrations by Jeff Kivett and Lynne Annette Clark

Published by Masters Press
A division of NTC/Contemporary Publishing Group, Inc.
4255 West Touhy Avenue, Lincolnwood (Chicago), Illinois 60712-1975 U.S.A.
Copyright © 1994 by Masters Press
Printed in the United States of America
International Standard Book Number: 0-940279-77-0
99 00 01 02 03 04 RCP 21 20 19 18 17 16 15 14 13 12 11 10 9 8 7 6 5 4 3

ACKNOWLEDGMENTS

I would like to thank the members of the Indianapolis Colts who posed for the interior photos in the book:

Carlos Etheridge

Kipp Vickers

Devon McDonald

Joe Staysniak

Brian Stablein

Brian Ratigan

Ron Solt

Orlando Lowry

Chris Gambol

Thanks also go to Masters Press, especially Mark Montieth, Tom Bast, and Holly Kondras, for their consistent persistence in pushing me through the writing of this book.

Finally, I would like to thank Dean Rockwell, who has been an inspiration to me throughout my competitive life.

DEDICATION

To my parents Gus and Mary. You showed me the way and fit me into my first workboots with love.

To my loving wife Carrie and my children, Katie, Jake and John Thomas. You are the wind beneath my wings.

TABLE OF CONTENTS

1. MOTIVATION: THE KEY TO SUCCESS...1

2. MYTHS ABOUT STRENGTH TRAINING.................................9

3. OVERCOMING INJURIES...19

4. IMPROVING YOUR FLEXIBILITY.................................23

5. CONCENTRATION DRILLS...39

6. PLYOMETRIC TRAINING...45

7. STRENGTH TRAINING EXERCISES.................................49

8. THE PROGRAM...83

9. THE DAILY OFF-SEASON SCHEDULE.................................99

10. NUTRITION...121

APPENDIX: PATTERN RUN PROGRESSIONS.................................125

FOREWORD

I remember well the first time I met Tom Zupancic. I left the meeting with the offensive line of the Indianapolis Colts and went to the temporary weight room. Hard rock music was blasting through the tiny gymnasium, and all eyes were riveted on the back of the room while our new strength and conditioning coach proceeded to bang his head on the cinder block wall, take a couple of snorts from an ammonia capsule, bless himself and then lie down and do repetitions with a 600-pound weight on the bench press. Little did I know that this man was about to take the Colts from the weakest team in the NFL to the strongest in just four years.

Tom Zupancic has done more than just strengthen the men who's lives he has touched. Over the ten years I worked with him, he fulfilled his dream of sharing what he has learned about success and motivation to help others achieve their goals and dreams. In addition to coaching hundreds of players, "Zup" has given motivational speeches to thousands of people in the community. During any given week, Zup might talk to a Boy Scout troop, speak at a local Exchange Club meeting, or visit schools; amazing kids and adults by lifting a car with his neck, having volunteers try to choke him (pretty tough to do to a guy with a 28-inch neck) and breaking bricks with his forehead.

Zup has been more than a coach to me and to others. He has been a father figure, brother and, most importantly, a good friend. Without his help, I would have been a good player. With his help, I benched over 500-pounds, squatted 810-pounds, and deadlifted 780-pounds. The strength and explosiveness that Zup helped me to develop enabled me to play 10 years in the NFL as an All-Pro Offensive Lineman. The work habits and dedication he instilled in me has helped me to become a better person and a success in the community. In addition to having owned three businesses, I am helping to coach a high school football, passing on what Zup has taught me. Whether you are a young athlete, a salesperson or the head of a company, this book will help you unlock your potential and inspire you to achieve your utmost success in life.

Ron Solt
Indianapolis Colts, 1984-1988
Philadelphia Eagles, 1988-1992
Indianapolis Colts, 1992-1994

1 MOTIVATION: THE KEY TO SUCCESS

Obstacles are those frightful things you see when you take your eyes off the goal

It is often said that the ability to motivate an athlete to reach his full potential is the key to coaching success. This has been stated countless times, in books and in seminars, and is widely accepted. But coaches who adhere to it religiously are mistaken.

The key to a successful program is motivating athletes to *motivate themselves* and to motivate their peers. If an athlete feels goal-oriented only when in the presence of a coach, then a coach's impact is at best minimal. An athlete who lives in a world in which he is self-motivated 24-hours a day has endless possibilities for success. The concept of becoming limitless can only be achieved through a consistent lifestyle of forward motion.

Coaches and athletes must remember that not everyone can be all-pro, all-state or even all-conference, and they should set their goals accordingly. Too many coaches believe they can take any player and turn him into a star. But in attempting to do so, they might ruin what might have been a "good" athlete. Coaches should evaluate personnel carefully before establishing goals for their athletes.

It also is important to remember that goal-setting and goal-reaching is not a twenty-minute-twice-per-week exercise. Coaches must spend a great deal of time with their athletes, counseling them on the proper techniques and helping them set realistic and achievable goals.

I have five insights into motivation that have been my mantra from the beginning. I know that they have helped me get where I am today, and I think they can help you too.

INSIGHT NO. 1 — SET GOALS – AND REACH THEM!

While training for the 1984 Olympic Games, I spent a month in Colorado Springs, Colorado at the Olympic Training Center. One day I wandered out onto the archery course. There was quite a commotion—television cameras, reporters, lots of people—all gathered around one archer.

Some people are like wheel-barrows: they stand still until they are pushed

This particular archer had won several national championships and world titles and was now preparing to go for an Olympic medal. Apparently he was also quite a hunter. He had in fact killed several large animals, including a bull elephant, with his bow and arrows. Because of obvious similarities between the elephant and me, I quickly became this man's friend.

The next statement you read may raise your brow. I believe I could take anyone reading this book and in ten minutes have you hitting a target more consistently than the champion archer. This might seem impossible given my lack of expertise as an archery teacher, but it could be done — with one stipulation: the archer would be blindfolded.

A ridiculous request? Of course. After all, how can an archer, no matter how talented, be expected to hit a target that he can't see? Impossible, right? Right. That is the point of the story. Just as it would be impossible for a champion archer to hit a target that he couldn't see, it is impossible for you to hit a goal that you don't envision. You have got to have goals in life if you want to reach your success potential.

INSIGHT NO. 2 — THE MOTIVATION

I believe the formula for success is a fairly simple equation:

GOAL + PLAN + MOTIVATION = SUCCESS

My analogy of the "You Train" is a clear explanation of this equation. Imagine that you are a train sitting in your hometown. Your destination (goal) is Chicago, Illinois. In order to reach Chicago, you need a train track from your town to Chicago. The track is your plan. Any railroad track must be held together and reinforced by railroad ties. The ties for the "You Train" track are "atta-boys." Everytime you pass over one of these ties you are closer to your goal of Chicago. The ties reach up as you move forward, slap you on the back and say "atta-boy." "Atta-boys" are your constant motivation to keep moving toward Chicago. Everytime you feel one, you know you are getting closer to your goal. The "atta-boy" ties are very important because they are a constant reminder of your forward progress.

The fuel for the "You Train" is a four-letter word that can ultimately stop the train short of Chicago if you don't put enough in. That word is WORK. Lack of work can stop you dead on the tracks. The "You Train," when traveling on a solid track (plan), reinforced by strong ties ("atta-boys"), and properly filled with fuel (work) will ultimately reach Chicago (your goal). The process of successfully reaching Chicago is simple, but not easy. It is simple in that you know where you want to go, how you are going to get there, and are excited about your eventual arrival. But it is not easy, because along the way you will have unscheduled stops, pitfalls, obstacles and setbacks.

INSIGHT NO. 3 - EVERYONE CAN REACH THE ULTIMATE SUCCESS IN LIFE

How, you ask, can everyone reach the pinnacle of success? After all, there can be only one best running back, one best lawyer, one best butcher, baker and candlestick maker. This is a true statement. On any given day, there can be only one best anyone at anything. The true measure of success is not necessarily being the best. True greatness, true genius and ultimate success come from being the best that you can be.

All of us have the seeds of greatness planted within. The nurturing of these seeds is our responsibility and ours alone. Set goals, make a specific plan and then work daily to reach those goals, no matter how difficult it might become. That's when you are on your way to becoming the ultimate success — the best you that you can be.

Many times on our road toward becoming the best we find ourselves in tough situations when progress toward our goal is slowed or temporarily stopped. It is tempting during tough times to blame someone else for our shortcomings. We've all done it at one time or another — pointed that blaming finger away from ourselves. "If it wasn't for my parents ... or my wife ... or my girlfriend ... or my coach ... or the offense ... or the defense ... or that fumble ... I would have been more successful. If this had not happened or that had not happened, my situation would be better. It was his fault, her fault, their fault—my hands are clean." It is so tempting, and so easy, to point the finger of blame elsewhere.

Fortunately, the finger of blame tells the truth, the whole truth and nothing but the truth. Unfortunately, the truth may not be what you want to hear.

This experiment explains what I mean. Point your index finger at something or someone in the room. Now imagine that that something or someone is truly responsible for your inability to reach your goals. Surely you can muster a lot of hostility and anger toward the object or person. How dare they keep you from being your best!

Now, stop and point that index finger again. This time, however, look at the entire hand. Notice that only one finger points at your object of blame. Now look at the other three fingers of that hand, because they tell the real story. These three fingers are pointing at the person who is really responsible for your situation in life. These fingers point directly at you. You and you alone are ultimately responsible for your success or failure in life.

Don't make excuses, don't try to point off blame; the fingers are accurate. Stop after a loss, setback or failure, re-group and take the proverbial bull by the horns. Reset your goals, re-fuel the "You Train," fix the plan and move on.

If you want to leave footprints in the sands of time, wear work shoes

A task

half done

is as

useless as

a task

never

begun

INSIGHT NO. 4 - NEVER ALLOW YOURSELF OR OTHERS TO PLACE LIMITS ON YOU

Negative thinking on a regular basis can cripple your efforts to be your best you. Combining negative thinking with listening to negative babble from friends, the family doctor, even so-called "experts" can multiply that crippling effect. If you are surrounded by totally positive people and never have any doubt in your ability to succeed in every endeavor you attempt, then you, my friend, are in a select minority. Most of us live in a world where negativity runs rampant. The newspaper, the evening news and countless daytime talk shows bombard us with every malady mankind can experience.

The key to overcoming this negative onslaught is to stay focused on your goals. Make up your mind what you want to accomplish, devise your plan and begin the trek with a single-minded conviction to succeed. Along the way, many might say it can't be done—you may even doubt yourself when times get tough—but remember, a well researched goal with a specific plan will work if you do. Think big, think smart, adjust on the move, believe in yourself and keep working. If you're going to be the best you can be, barriers, both real and imagined, must come down.

While I was preparing for the 1984 Olympics, my coach, a Russian defector, told a group of us an interesting story about barriers. Harry Houdini, the great magician and escape artist, had accomplished many amazing feats in his career. One of the things Houdini was famous for was his ability to break out of a jail cell. Any jail cell. He had attempted this feat hundreds of times and had never failed. One day, a small town in England issued a challenge to Houdini. This small town claimed to have a jail from which Houdini could not escape. To back their claim, they offered Houdini $10,000 if he successfully escaped from it. The challenge was accepted confidently by Houdini and a date was set.

When Houdini rolled into town, he was greeted by a parade in his honor that was the biggest the town had ever seen. Houdini strolled confidently through the crowd and up the stairs of the new jail. The only stipulation was that Houdini be searched, put in a cell and left alone for one hour to attempt his escape. He was led to the cell and searched from head to toe.

When the officials were satisfied that Houdini was not concealing any devices to aid his escape, he was placed in the cell. The cell door was closed, and the one-hour countdown began.

Houdini reached inside his belt buckle, removed a small piece of flexible steel and immediately went to work on the lock. Houdini had a very confident smirk on his face as he twisted and turned the lock. Many times before he had been able to escape so quickly that he would actually follow his challengers out of the room. This time, though, Houdini was having difficulty. Ten, fifteen, twenty minutes went by and Houdini was still working feverishly to escape. At the half-hour mark, the confident expression on Houdini's face was replaced by a genuine look of concern. In hundreds of previously successful escapes, none had ever taken this long. But Houdini continued to work. Forty minutes, fifty minutes, fifty-five minutes. In five more minutes, Houdini would fail for the first time in his career. Losing the $10,000 was bad enough, but Houdini shuddered at the thought of his first failure. The minutes continued to pass. Finally, at 59 minutes, Houdini, drenched in sweat and totally exhausted, collapsed against the cell door ... AND IT SWUNG OPEN.

Why? THE DOOR HAD NEVER BEEN LOCKED! The jail officials knew Houdini could open a locked cell door, so they hadn't locked it. The door was locked in one place and one place only: in Houdini's mind. And by being locked in his mind, it was locked as tightly as if the hundred best locksmiths in the world had slapped their best locks on it.

The point our coach was trying to make was that what we believe controls what we achieve. Whether you are trying to win an Olympic title, bench press 600 pounds, or simply striving to be the best you can be, your chance of success is dictated by how you think. Henry Ford said, "If you think you can, or think you can't, you're probably right."

If, in your pursuit of personal excellence, you happen to run into a cell door, don't check it to see if it is locked, don't call out for help to open it, don't turn and walk away. When you reach that cell door along your track — and you will — lower your shoulder and break it down. No barrier is strong enough to keep you from becoming your best unless you allow it to be.

INSIGHT NO. 5 - NEVER LET YOURSELF GET AWAY WITH JUST GETTING BY

Mediocre, according to Webster's Dictionary, is defined as "of moderate or low quality: ordinary." Classifying yourself as mediocre can mean that you are presently a total success or a miserable failure. How can this be? If, with hard work, careful planning, and constant and focused adjusting, you end up reaching mediocre as the best you that you can be, then you are a success. If, on the other hand, you are mediocre or ordinary, and you never work, plan or focus on reaching your rung on the ladder of your best you, then, my friend, you are currently a failure.

The measuring stick of success doesn't have inches, centimeters or feet. The measuring stick of success is you. How close you come to filling out you is truly the standard for success. Conceive, believe and achieve. If the best "yous" settled for mediocre, world records wouldn't be recorded and/or broken.

One of the most incredible world records ever broken was the four-minute barrier in the mile. For years, athletes the world over were searching for the key to break that seemingly impossible barrier. Runners, coaches and even doctors seemed to accept the

The mind is its own place and in itself can make a heaven of hell – or a hell of heaven

impossibility of breaking the four-minute barrier. Milers would show up at races all over the world, trying to break a barrier most of them were convinced could not be broken. All the negative "bricks" weighed them down and influenced their self-image.

The doubt and limitations seemed insurmountable until the arrival of Roger Bannister, a British runner. Bannister didn't allow the failures of past great milers, the babbling of negative coaches or the medical opinions of doctors to affect what he firmly believed he would accomplish. On May 6, 1954, Bannister burst through this long-standing barrier by finishing a mile in 3 minutes, 59.4 seconds.

Bannister removed the negative bricks from milers all over the world that day. In the months that followed, runners broke the four-minute barrier consistently — because the barrier was a mental one, not a physical one.

Competitors must realize that they are limitless beings. Scientists claim we use only about five percent of our brain's capabilities on a regular basis. Think of the untapped power! The key to unlocking that power is to accept yourself as a deserving, hard working, driven individual whom you dearly love. Don't allow the negative bricks of others to become part of your self-image, and never allow yourself to build a wall with negative bricks. Climb your mountain and constantly reach for your best you.

IT TAKES ALL KINDS

Successful teams are made up of successful individuals. But a team includes more types of personalities than it does positions. To motivate these various individuals, a coach must understand where each is coming from. Blanket motivation for an entire team is, at best, marginally effective. A coach must try to find the "button" on as many players as possible to motivate them. The at-large team goal to win must also be each individual's goal.

The tactics used to help each individual reach that common goal vary greatly. The following list of player types covers a variety of personality traits. Some players fit squarely into one category. Others have traits of two or more.

A coach who is unsure where his players fit on the list should get to know them better. Coaches scout their opponents extensively; they should make it a point to know and understand their own players first.

The following are some of the personality types that can be found on any team. Coaches can use it to help identify their players' personalities and understand them better. Players can study it to see where they fit in, and determine what changes they need to make in themselves to become more productive.

Mr. Overachiever: A person with limited athletic ability who, through hard work and hustle, gets every ounce out of what he has. This type of person often plays "over his head" in games where hustle and tenacity make the difference.

Mr. Natural: A person blessed with instinct, speed, quickness and strength. Mr. Natural will often tend to have poor training habits because of his ability to perform well without training.

Mr. Golden Boy: A person with the talents of Mr. Natural and the tenacity of Mr. Overachiever. They are rare commodities, and highly valued.

Mr. Know It All: A person who thinks he has all the answers. This type of person is very difficult to motivate or coach because he never really believes in someone else's system. He usually does have all the answers — but, unfortunately, they don't always match the coach's questions.

Mr. Non-Urgent: A person who has the tools needed for success but no fire in the furnace. He usually maintains a very even, low profile and never gets excited by the sting of competition.

Mr. Anti-All: A person who has the ability to become the coach's biggest headache. If he has talent and is valuable, then a coach can find himself defending every move the coach makes. This player will inevitably find fault with the coach's philosophy and pull some of his teammates his way.

Mr. Normal Norm: The majority of people fall into this category. They are the normal Joes who can be motivated to achieve desired goals, and they make up the foundation of your organization.

Mr. Hooray For Me: A person who is out for Numero Uno. He is easy to motivate as long as the eventual outcome benefits him. But selfishness is not a desirable quality in a team effort.

Mr. Pressure: A person most likely to be an average player, but a player for all the wrong reasons. He is participating because of family or peer pressure, and is therefore attempting to achieve someone else's goals rather than his own.

Mr. I Think I'm A Ten: A person with an exaggerated, unrealistic view of his talent. It's almost as if he looks in the mirror and sees something that is not there. Mr. I Think I'm A Ten is probably only a five, but good luck convincing him of that.

There are no hopeless situations — only people who have grown hopeless about them

THE MIRROR TEST

Competitors — and this includes athletes and coaches —should look at themselves in a mirror occasionally and appraise the person they see. If you are not as successful as you would like to be, you should look yourself in the eye and ask questions. Am I asserting myself? Am I lazy? Have I set realistic goals for myself? Am I dedicated toward reaching these goals? Am I doing everything I can to improve myself? If not, why?

This exercise works better than a lie detector because it's difficult to look yourself in the eye and lie. The first step toward becoming successful is to be honest with your best friend: yourself. If you do not believe you are your own best friend, go back and look in the mirror. You dress, wash, feed, groom, share good times with, share bad times with, are sick with, vacation with, share your deepest secrets with, work with, sleep with, drink with and LIVE with yourself. To be successful in life, you must first be honest with and totally love yourself.

2 MYTHS ABOUT STRENGTH TRAINING

It is better to understand a little than to misunderstand a lot

Many myths surround strength training. They are beliefs that have persisted throughout the years despite scientific research that proves them to be false. For many people, they are nothing more than excuses not to work out.

The following are some of the more common myths.

1. "As soon as you stop working out, all that muscle will turn to fat."

This statement, usually made by someone looking for an excuse not to train, is totally false. Muscle will not turn to fat any more than a diamond will turn into a two-by-four. Fat and muscle are two completely different physiological elements.

If a formerly muscular person does become fat, it is simply because that person stops working out, causing the muscles to atrophy, but continues eating the same amount of calories. The excess calories cause the body fat to increase, not the lack of working out. If a person reduces or ceases his workouts, all he has to do to avoid gaining fat is reduce his caloric intake.

Muscle is a "use it or lose it" proposition. You must exert greater, or at the very least consistent, demands on your muscles or they will become weaker and smaller. The body has priorities in utilizing its nutrients. Twenty-inch arms are not at the top of the list unless you demand, by training, that a muscle be big and strong.

2. "I would work out, but I don't want to look like a muscle-bound freak."

This also is a statement spoken by someone who is looking for an excuse not to work out. When I first opened a gymnasium, this was a concern of many of my prospective clients. I would assure them that I would design a program for their individual goals and

You teach

more with

your life

than with

your lips

needs, and that we would only let them reach their desired "big-ness." As the years passed, my approach changed considerably. My new approach was rather callous, and probably wouldn't be taught in any salesmanship seminars. It went as follows:

Customer: "I want to work out, but I don't want to look like one of those muscle-bound freaks you see on TV."

Me (with genuine concern in my eyes): "Partner, let me assure you that if you moved into this gym, worked out 24 hours a day, took steroids, ate, drank and slept weight lifting for one solid year, you still won't look like the `freaks' you see on TV." Then I would smile, pat them on the back, and proceed to give them my per-sonal plan, personal goal, control-your-bigness routine.

My point is this: if you are an NFL player, you train muscle for that sport. You train specific muscles that help you become bigger, stronger and more explosive. If you are a Joe-bag-o-donuts who wants to tone your body so you look good in a bathing suit, your training program will be much different. The bottom line is that muscle doesn't uncontrollably appear on your body for no reason. You customize the program to fit your goals and needs. Your train-ing, diet and lifestyle dictate how quickly you reach those goals. An athlete training for football, or anyone for that matter, won't become a "freak" unless their goal is to become a "freak" —and even then it is very difficult and rare. Why do you think you see them on TV?

3. "If I work out, I won't be able to swing a golf club, shoot a basketball, or throw a baseball."

This statement is common among uninformed athletes. The be-lief that you will lose touch with other athletic skills by lifting weights has been disproven time and time again. Nearly every NBA team has both an off-season and an in-season weight strength program. Baseball has incorporated strength training as well, with impres-sive results for pitchers and hitters. Professional golfers are follow-ing conditioning programs to strengthen often-used and often-in-jured muscles.

The key element in setting up a workout program to improve your performance in any sport is to include practice of your skills with your workouts. Studies have shown that if you cease practic-ing your particular athletic skills and only lift weights, your skills will diminish faster than if you did nothing at all. However, if your workouts include specific skill practice along with weight training, the ability to execute those skills improves. It stands to reason that a stronger, well-conditioned muscle will enable a skill movement to be executed with less effort and for an extended period of time before fatigue sets in. At the top of every professional sport you will find the best athletes participating in a strength and condition-ing program designed to enhance their particular athletic skills. Remember, a well-conditioned body can perform better, longer and with less chance of injury.

4. "If I work out, I'll become slower with the added muscle size and weight."

This belief can quickly be refuted by running off names such as Carl Lewis, Ben Johnson, Bo Jackson, Florence Griffith-Joyner and Evelyn Ashford. All of them are world class sprinters and train extensively with weights. This is obvious by their lean muscled appearance. Speed is important in almost every athletic endeavor. The quest to improve speed is an ongoing process for athletes everywhere.

Weight training has emerged as a major factor in achieving that quest. It is now commonly accepted that a stronger muscle is a faster muscle over a short distance. Certainly this would apply in football. The combination of weight training and flexibility exercises and proper running form are crucial ingredients in improving speed. The ability to squat 800 pounds will do little to improve a football player's speed if he does not practice proper running form and flexibility training.

Again, football players must take part in a program specific to their needs. It would be drastically different than that used by a marathon runner, a baseball player or a bodybuilder. The sets, reps and even the exercises are different, but weight training still plays an important role.

CREATING A MOOD

Another weight training myth is one commonly held by coaches and P.E. instructors. Coaches often think a weight room should be a sparse, drab place decorated with nothing but sweat and blood. That's wrong! It's important to create an environment that is clean, pleasing and, most of all, energetic. This isn't a place for athletes to go to study, relax or just hang out. This is a place to get stronger, get better, and gain confidence. The atmosphere should be aggressive, even a little volatile. Every exercise needs to be attacked, so the mood must reflect that.

Savvy interior decorating can help. Color schemes are important. Stay away from soft pastels and go for strong, bold colors. Even if your school or team colors are rather ordinary, you can use stronger colors as accents. If necessary, invest in a few gallons of paint and have the athletes paint the room themselves; it will make the room that much more special to them.

The room should contain several mirrors. Some coaches believe mirrors are for sissies who want to admire themselves all the time, but it's really a form of motivation. The athletes can see the rewards of their hard work and get "pumped up" about getting pumped up.

Athletes, in fact, should be encouraged to look in the mirror so they can monitor their progress and benefit from the positive feedback. Although a lifting program for football is a power program with a practical application, rather than a bodybuilding program

Don't brag; it isn't the whistle that pulls the train

designed to sculpt the body, the athlete's body still will change in positive ways. He will get bigger, stronger and look better. If checking his progress and admiring the changes in the mirror motivates him to work harder, great!

Music also helps set the mood. This isn't the place for Sinatra or Streisand. You want loud, aggressive music that older coaches probably won't like. Young athletes should have some leeway here, because the kind of music they like probably is perfect for the atmosphere that should be established in a weight room.

If disputes arise over what type of music to play, a system should be set up. The strongest player can choose, which might be another means of motivation, although that might not be fair to the smaller players. Perhaps a rotation can be established whereby every team member takes a turn deciding which music plays. Regardless, make it part of the overall program and try to find a way to link it with motivation.

It's also important to have an abundance of trash cans in the room, because if the athletes are truly working hard some of them are going to throw up occasionally. This is a cause for celebration, not concern, as long as they aren't sick, hurt or dehydrated. Nothing motivates an athlete more than to see a teammate vomit from having worked so hard. This is peer pressure at its best.

The layout of the weight room also should be changed once a month or so to give it a fresh look, just as with rearranging the furniture in your house. The coach should do it over the weekend so that the players are surprised when they walk in on Monday. It's a nuisance to do, but it will give the players a new vitality during their workouts.

A weight room's wall space should be used to display the accomplishments of the athletes. A total program with specific goals should be mapped out at the beginning, and the players should be held accountable at various times during the year through testing. Put charts on the wall that show everyone's progress; this is another form of peer pressure. It's important, however, for athletes and coaches alike to understand that lifting the most weight doesn't necessarily indicate success. The point is for each athlete to come as close as possible to fulfilling his potential.

That's the strength coach's primary job: motivating the athletes to reach their potential. Young athletes train for different reasons — to be better players, to look good for the girls, to feel more macho, all sorts of things. Whatever works for them is OK as long as they make the kind of progress they need to make to become better football players.

The coach should create an atmosphere in the weight room in which an athlete can hone his competitive edge. A coach — or one of the players, for that matter — can take a player aside and ask how come so-and-so is doing better than he is. Small battles should be created in the weight room between players of similar size, or between a player and the equipment. If a player can win 300 battles in the weight room during the off-season, he's that much more prepared to fight the battles on the field because he's accustomed to putting himself on the line.

WORKING HARD AND HAVING FUN

Let's face it, football is controlled violence. It's violence within a set of rules. At the higher levels, the players are hitting each other at high rates of speed with an impact that is beyond the imagination of most people. At any level, it's a game that demands peak conditioning. If an athlete is stronger and more durable because of a conditioning program, he will perform better and suffer fewer injuries. At the professional level, he can extend his career because of his work in the weight room.

But there's more. A conditioning program lifts an athlete's self-image and gives him confidence. This can be particularly beneficial in the fourth quarter when the game is on the line. If an athlete knows he is better conditioned than his opponent, he has a better chance to win close games in the fourth quarter. Just knowing he is better conditioned should help him perform better.

It doesn't matter that much whether an athlete can bench press 330 pounds instead of 300 pounds, or squat 450 pounds instead of 400 pounds. What matters more, particularly at the younger levels of play, is that the athletes emerge from a training program feeling good about themselves. When they are turned loose by the strength coach, they should feel as if they are the toughest, meanest S.O.B.s out there, that nobody has worked harder than they have, and that they DESERVE to win.

Motivation is always the greatest challenge, both for the coaches and the players. The athletes must be self-motivated for the most part, but a coach can help. With a little creativity, a coach can organize a few fun events and award prizes — nothing extravagant, just something to keep everyone's interest high. Even professional athletes get excited about small prizes. They may be millionaires, but they'll run through a wall for a T-shirt or a trophy when competing against their peers, because some things can't be bought.

A coach, for example, can start a 1,000-pound club (or a lesser weight that is appropriate for younger athletes) and give T-shirts to those who reach the goal in the squat, bench press and dead lift.

Or, with a little imagination, a coach can come up with something truly unique and fun that will motivate his athletes to work hard. With the Indianapolis Colts, we have an Iron Man competition every summer that has really caught on. The competition is divided into three weight divisions: less than 200 pounds, 200-250 pounds, and more than 250 pounds. All the players compete in the same events, but only against those in their weight division.

If you

aim at

nothing

you will

hit it

everytime

A hammer

breaks

glass but

forges steel

Our Iron Man contest consists of the following events:

1. **Hay bale carry.** Place a 70-pound bale of hay on a 100-yard field. The athlete picks up the bale and carries it the length of the field as fast as he can. Best time wins. You can use more than one bale to speed up the competition.

2. **Rock toss.** Place a 50-pound rock within a 10-foot circle. Each player gets two throws. Best distance wins.

3. **Sand pit obstacle.** Five 25-pound rocks are placed one yard apart. Each player throws the rocks over a line 10 yards away, then jumps into a pit that is 70 yards long and filled two feet deep with sand and sprints to the end, circles a cone, and sprints back to the start/finish line. Best time wins.

4. **300-yard shuttle.** Each player picks up a 120-pound punching bag and carries it through six 50-yard dashes — down and back, down and back, down and back. Best time wins.

5. **Tire toss.** Each player throws a large truck tire from within a 10-foot circle. Longest throw wins.

6. **Truck push.** Each athlete pushes a pickup truck. Those weighing under 200 pounds push it 40 yards; those weighing 200-250 pounds push it 50 yards, and those weighing more than 250 pounds push it 60 yards. Best time wins.

Adversity

causes

some men

to break –

others to

break

records

When it

comes to

doing

things for

others –

some people

stop at

nothing

The competition has a lighthearted atmosphere, but you would be amazed by the intensity. An event such as this should be conducted at the finish of a pre-season conditioning program. It's the perfect way to cap off a session, because we follow it with a huge picnic.

Trophies are awarded to the top three finishers in each weight division. The third-place finishers get a 24-inch trophy, second-place finishers get a 30-inch trophy and the first-place finishers get a 36-inch trophy. The overall champion goes home with a 46-inch trophy.

Believe me, players at all levels take these competitions seriously. I'll never forget the time I visited Steve Emtman, a defensive tackle who was the No. 1 overall pick in the 1992 NFL draft, when he was recovering at home from knee surgery. Emtman had won all sorts of prestigious honors during his high school and college football career. But on his fireplace mantel, prominently displayed amid all his hardware, was his 46-inch Iron Man trophy.

Another time a rookie who had performed well in our Iron Man competition took his trophy with him to his contract negotiation with management as a means of supporting his bid for a higher salary.

You don't have to offer large trophies, however. Almost anything will do. The idea is to have a competition that gives everyone a chance to be reasonably successful. If you award a key chain it will be cherished forever, because it represents a lot of hard work and accomplishment for the athlete.

Competitions don't have to be as elaborate as our Iron Man. Before I joined the NFL, I owned and operated Zupancic's Gym in Indianapolis, Indiana. Many of the football players who trained there were from Roncalli High School. As part of their training, I had them push an old car up and down the parking lot. As the season approached, I met with the seniors about a good way to cap off the off-season. It was decided that the entire team would meet at the gym at 5 a.m. on the last Sunday before their training camp began. We figured that they would have to win 14 games to win the Indiana State Football Championship. The plan was to push that old car they had been training with all year one mile for each game they needed to win.

We divided the team into groups of three people (pushers) and began the 14 mile push. Each group would push the car 1/2 mile while the rest of the team jogged along side for support. Parents were there to watch and provide drinks; coaches came to add their support, and the cheerleaders decorated the car with school colors.

The first seven or eight miles of that 14 mile trip seemed to fly by, the players were excited and light-hearted, and a pep rally atmosphere was present. At about mile nine, the reality of the 14 mile trip set in. People began to hit the wall, the chatter ceased and suddenly this little jaunt became a real challenge. Some of the less conditioned players were moaning and threatening to call it quits. This is when the leaders of the team stepped up, coaxed, pushed, and in some cases, actually carried the moaners through the rest of the journey.

That group of high school football players had set out to push a car 14 miles that Sunday morning and the wheels never stopped rolling until the job was done. They were greeted at the finish line by students, teachers and boosters of the team with thunderous applause reminiscent of the Olympic marathon finish.

Roncalli High School won the state title that year – not because of what the did that Sunday morning, but because they had become a *team*. The players, coaches and fans demonstrated an indomitable spirit before the season ever began. That spirit grew throughout the year and enabled them to reach their goal.

Creative, demanding events such as an Iron Man competition or pushing a car, help build that mysterious chemistry that holds a team together through the good times and bad. These memorable events are a shared experience, the type all good families enjoy, that tightens the bond. Thirty years later, when the players get together for reunions, they'll still talk about the time they pushed a car along the road at 5 a.m. They also help break up the drudgery of the workouts all athletes must endure to achieve their potential. If they're allowed to have some fun, they'll enjoy the journey that much more.

Triumph

is just

"umph"

added

to try

3 OVERCOMING INJURIES

The harder we get knocked down, the higher we bounce

During my 10 years in the NFL, I've had many experiences with players regarding their conditioning program. I've seen players bounce back from a serious injury in half the time their doctors predicted because of their dedication in the weight room. I've seen players who prolonged their careers a couple of years past the norm because of their conditioning program. I've seen players who wouldn't have even earned a roster spot if not for their training habits. Unfortunately, I've also seen a few players who never quite achieved their potential because they didn't work as hard as they could have.

Although a good conditioning program reduces the risk of injury, it does not prevent it. Football is a violent game, and injuries are bound to occur. But athletes who have worked hard to condition themselves will bounce back from an injury faster than those who haven't. Not only are they able to withstand the punishment better, but they have an ingrained knowledge of their bodies and what they can do to overcome their injuries.

Ron Solt, an All-Pro guard who played for the Colts and Eagles, virtually made and extended his career because of his tenacious attitude toward conditioning. Ron was able to work through serious knee and shoulder injuries and rejuvinate his body for each season. When he was unable to train, Ron's weight would drop to the mid-260s, too light to play in the NFL. Through a total committment to all facets of his program, he was able to maintain 270 pounds at 10 percent body fat throughout his career.

Joe Klecko, who played for the Colts and the New York Jets, earned All-Pro honors at three positions: nose guard, defensive tackle, and defensive end. Throughout his career, Joe experienced a multitude of injuries that for someone else could have been career ending. Joe's dedication and work habits along with the knowledge he had gained through years of lifting experience enabled him to overcome the injuries and continue his brilliant career.

If you do not enjoy what you have, how can you be happy with more?

Will Wolford signed with the Colts after earning All-Pro honors with the Buffalo Bills. Will suffered a serious injury to his rotator cuff in Buffalo's 1993 Super Bowl loss to the Dallas Cowboys.After Will's surgery, the prognosis was that he might miss most or all of the following season. Will did what the doctor's thought couldn't be done. He cut his rehab time in half and was ready for the 1993 season opener. Will had a dogged determination in his rehab program. He set his sights on the opening game and through hard work accomplished his goal. I have seen a lot of tough people throughout the years, but Will would definitely be at the top of the list. He endured workouts that most men would not, or could not, endure and kept coming back for more.

Jeff Herrod, a linebacker for the Colts, accomplished a similar feat. He dislocated an ankle during a preseason game in 1993, a severe injury that normally forces athletes into eight to ten weeks of inactivity. But as he was being driven off the field in the back of the cart with his toe almost pointing down, his first comment was "I'll be back in half the time they say it will take." He didn't know the extent of his injuries at the time, but he knew how hard he was willing to work and how much pain he was able to withstand.

Steve Emtman was virtually injury-free until he tore his anterior cruciate ligament during his rookie year in 1992. He set out on a vigorous rehab program that included countless hours with the trainers doing monotonous stretching and flexion work to regain his full range of motion. He had to complete all of this work before he could even begin the off-season program that would enable him to begin his second NFL season.

In the beginning, weights that had been warmups for him suddenly became maximum efforts. However, calling on the knowledge that he had achieved much greater weights before enabled him to push through the pain and discomfort. Before entering training camp, he was the strongest he had ever been in his life.

Emtman suffered another major injury early in the 1993 season, but don't count him out. Some people participate in a program; Emtman takes a program over and challenges it.

Athletes who condition properly learn to recognize the difference between "good" pain and "bad" pain while rehabilitating. Good pain is the normal fatigue and discomfort that comes from working the muscles. Bad pain can lead to further injury to an existing problem. It might be a specific discomfort in a ligament, tendon or joint rather than general soreness. These athletes also are able to recognize the fine line between training hard and overtraining. This comes through experience and knowledge.

MOTIVATING THE INJURED ATHLETE

Motivating an injured athlete is a complicated process. Any injury can be a career-ending blow — if not physically, mentally. Young athletes in particular have a difficult time coming back from injuries, and might become discouraged enough to quit if they are not properly guided by a coach or trainer.

Take, for example, the case of Ed, a star halfback on a high school football team. During a practice session Ed gets hit in the knee and goes down. The coach meets Ed and his family at the hospital and learns they want to have orthoscopic surgery on the knee. Simple procedure, right? Wrong. Ed's mother is crying and she makes clear her feelings: "I never wanted him to play football. I knew something like this was going to happen. I've heard of other boys on the team getting hurt, so he must not have been properly supervised." By now Dad is sympathizing with Mom to save his marriage, because he's the one who let Ed participate in the first place.

The end result is that the coach has to deal with two distraught parents, not to mention find another halfback whose parents don't think the coach is a demon. What's a coach to do? After the smoke has cleared and it becomes obvious that little Eddie will walk again, it's time to work on the source of the coach's problem: educating the parents on the positive aspects of athletic participation.

Ed is part of a team that respects him and counts on him to contribute to the group's success. He is learning important lessons in discipline and pride. Overcoming adversity — in this case an injury — and rising to compete again is a lesson that will last throughout Ed's life.

The coach's job is to convince Ed and his parents that getting back on the playing field is the best thing for Ed and his character development. As for Ed, he has the challenge of making a complete recovery and getting back on the field. Orthoscopic surgery usually requires three or four weeks of rest and treatment before an athlete can resume normal contact. Some athletes, even at the professional level, have undergone this surgery in the preseason and not returned all season.

Why? In a word, pain. We've all heard the saying, "You've got to play with pain," but it's easier said than done. When an athlete experiences an injury and it alters his normal and comfortable range of motion, he can't be expected to play all out with pain. Coaches and parents must understand that an intruder has entered his life, and that intruder is pain. That pain will always be there to some degree. It's a learning process for the athlete to identify, accept and live with this new "partner."

Learning to play with pain is a matter of toughness, both mental and physical. Unfortunately, there is no pain meter to tell the athlete when to stop. As a coach, patience and understanding are key ingredients in helping the athlete return to the field.

What we accomplish is never as important as what we had to overcome to accomplish it

4 IMPROVING YOUR FLEXIBILITY

People who really get things done in this world are those who drive past the first layer of fatigue

The flexibility program is a vital part of your daily training routine. Combine flexibility, strength, and speed and you have the ingredients of success.

Each stretch has two phases:

1. **Easy Stretch Phase** — During this portion of the stretch, no discomfort should be felt in the stretching muscle.

2. **Developmental Stretch Phase** — During this portion, the muscle should be stretched to the point of slight burning.

Remember that all stretches should be held, **not bounced**, in the stretch position, and you must breathe evenly. Don't hold your breath.

The benefits from following a regular flexibility program are all very positive:

1. Provides players with more power through a fuller range of motion.

2. Reduces the chance of injuries caused by joints and muscle pulls.

3. Improves fluidity of motion which allows for greater speed.

4. Reduces soreness after strenuous activity.

5. Increases the blood flow to warm up muscles before activity.

6. Relieves tension.

The keenest pain comes from remembering what you should do a day too late to do it

23

NECK FLEXIBILITY EXERCISE

Easy Stretch Phase:

Rotate head in a circle; first to the right for eight seconds, then to the left for eight seconds.

Developmental Stretch Phase:

Look for 10 seconds over the right shoulder

Look for 10 seconds over the left shoulder

Look up for 10 seconds

Look down for 10 seconds

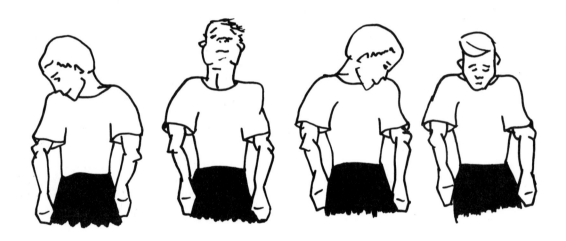

TRICEP, LAT AND SHOULDER FLEXIBILITY EXERCISE

Easy Stretch Phase:

With the arms extended overhead, hold the elbow of one arm with the hand of the other arm and exhale slowly for five seconds. Gently pull down on the elbow. Change arms and repeat.

Developmental Stretch Phase:

While repeating the above described motion, pull the elbow down until you feel a stretch and hold it for 15 seconds. Repeat with the other arm.

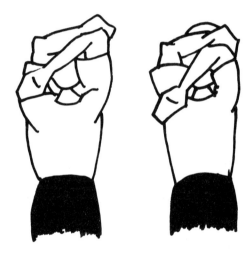

OUTER ARMS, RIBS AND SHOULDERS FLEXIBILITY EXERCISE

Easy Stretch Phase:

With arms up and palms together, as illustrated below, stretch arms upward and hold for 10 seconds.

Developmental Stretch Phase:

From the same position as the above description, reach up and slightly back. Hold for 15 seconds. Breathe normally.

LOWER BACK, GLUTES AND HAMSTRINGS FLEXIBILITY EXERCISE

Easy Stretch Phase:

With the feet shoulder width apart, point the toes straight ahead and bend the knees (one inch). Relax the arms, head and shoulders, bend at the waist and lower to an "easy" stretch position for 15 seconds.

Developmental Stretch Phase:

From the same position, reach forward and try to grab toes. Pull for 20 seconds.

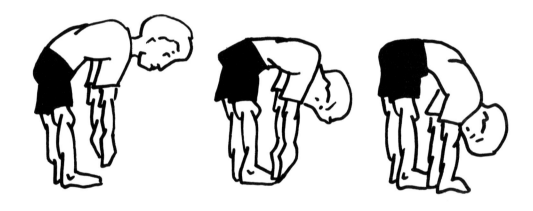

QUADS, KNEES, BACK AND DEEP GROIN FLEXIBILITY EXERCISE

Easy Stretch Phase:

With the feet about one foot apart and the toes pointed out, execute a deep knee bend with the elbows inside the knees. Relax for 20 seconds.

Developmental Stretch Phase:

From the same position, force the elbows into the knees and squat more deeply, spreading the legs farther apart. Hold for 30 seconds.

Easy

Developmental

LOWER BACK AND ERECTORS FLEXIBILITY EXERCISE

Easy Stretch Phase:

Not applicable

Developmental Stretch Phase:

Grasp both knees and roll back to the shoulders then up to the sitting position. Repeat eight times.

LOWER BACK, HAMSTRINGS AND GLUTES FLEXIBILITY EXERCISE

Easy Stretch Phase:

Lie on your back and grab one knee. Pull the knee slowly toward your chest keeping the other leg straight. Hold "easy" stretch each leg for 15 seconds.

Developmental Stretch Phase:

From the same position, pull the knee to the chest hard and hold each leg for 20 seconds.

LOWER BACK AND HIPS FLEXIBILITY EXERCISE

Easy Stretch Phase:

While lying on your back, bend your right knee to a 90 degree angle while keeping the opposite leg straight. Extend the right arm on the floor to your right. Relax for 15 seconds. Repeat the exercise with the left leg and arm.

Developmental Stretch Phase:

From the the same position, try to push the bent right knee down to the ground while touching the right elbow to the ground on the opposite side. Hold for 20 seconds. Repeat to the left.

QUADRICEP FLEXIBILITY EXERCISE

Easy Stretch Phase:

Lie on your left side and reach back for the right foot. Pull slightly and hold for 15 seconds. Repeat the exercise to the opposite side.

Developmental Stretch Phase:

From the same position, pull the foot back and allow the thigh to bend back from the hip. Arch the hip forward and hold for 20 seconds. Repeat the exercise with the other leg.

HAMSTRING, GLUTES AND HIPS FLEXIBILITY EXERCISE

Easy Stretch Phase:

Lie flat on your back and grasp the right foot with the left hand. With the right hand on the right knee, gently pull the leg toward the chest for 15 seconds. Repeat with the left leg.

Developmental Stretch Phase:

From the same position, pull with both hands until the stretch is felt in the upper hamstring and glutes. Hold for 20 seconds. Repeat with the other leg.

UPPER BACK, LOWER BACK, RIBS AND HIPS FLEXIBILITY EXERCISE

Easy Stretch Phase:

Sit with your right leg straight. Bend your left leg, cross your left foot over and rest it outside your right knee. Then bend the right elbow and rest it on the outside of the upper left thigh just above the knee. Look over the left shoulder for 15 seconds. Repeat to the other side.

Developmental Stretch Phase:

From the same position, use the elbow to torque the stretch as you look over the shoulder 20 seconds on each side.

GROIN FLEXIBILITY EXERCISE

Easy Stretch Phase:

Sit on the floor with the knees bent and the feet together and relax the legs for 20 seconds.

Developmental Stretch Phase:

Place elbows on the inside of the knees and force down for 20 seconds.

BACK, HAMSTRING AND GROIN FLEXIBILITY EXERCISE

Easy Stretch Phase:

Sit on the floor with the legs spread wide. Keep the legs straight and bend at the hips looking toward and reaching for the right and then the left ankle. Hold "easy" stretch 15 seconds on each leg.

Developmental Stretch Phase:

Reach with the left hand to the outside of the right foot and pull for 20 seconds. Repeat to the other leg.

Easy

Developmental

HAMSTRING, HIPS AND GROIN FLEXIBILITY EXERCISE

Easy Stretch Phase:

Fold left leg into the body while keeping the right leg straight with the toes pointed up. Keep your back straight and pull the toe or ankle slightly for 15 seconds. Repeat with the other leg.

Developmental Stretch Phase:

Bending from the hips with the back straight, pull toward the foot until a stretch is felt. Hold for 20 seconds. Repeat with the other leg.

5 CONCENTRATION DRILLS

Keep in step with your best self and you need never worry about the rest of the parade

The following workout consists of motor movement drills designed to improve neuromuscular pathways involved in the execution of football skills. *The workout is not intended to be a physical conditioning session. Concentration* and *maximum effort* are the keys in these drills. Therefore, the session is short and the rest periods between repetitions are adequate for complete recovery.

Research has shown that weight training, explosive training, and power training alone do little to precipitate actual football skills. However, research further indicates that weight training coupled with skill practice produces a dramatic positive effect in the skill practiced.

The following drills are as much mental as they are physical. They should be completed on the days outlined on your daily calendar and should *always be preceded by your flexibility routine.* You will find these drills to be a good warm-up for your lifting session.

TOTAL TIME — 10 minutes 35 seconds

ACTIVE TIME — 2 minutes 50 seconds

REST TIME — 7 minutes 45 seconds

EQUIPMENT UTILIZED

- Stop watch
- 6" step or block
- 6" block or hurdle

Dedication is more important than ability, but when you have both... success is yours

Failure

doesn't

mean you

will never

succeed;

it just

means it

will take

longer

DRILL #1 – STEPS UP ON 6" STEP

A. Right foot up followed by left up, then right down, left down.	15 seconds	
	Rest 30 seconds	
B. Left foot up followed by right up, then left down, right down.	15 seconds	
	Rest 60 seconds	
C. Hop up and down-both feet	15 seconds	
	Rest 60 seconds	

DRILL #2 – SIDE HURDLE SPEED HOPS

A. Both feet	15 seconds
	Rest 30 seconds
B. Both feet	15 seconds
	Rest 30 seconds
C. Both feet	15 seconds
	Rest 60 seconds

DRILL #3 – LOW FEET AND HAND CHOP (RAPID LOW STEP RUN IN PLACE)

A. Start	15 seconds
	Rest 30 seconds
B. Start	15 seconds
	Rest 60 seconds

DRILL #4 – HIGH KNEE AND HAND (RAPID HIGH STEP RUN IN PLACE)

A. Start	10 seconds
	Rest 30 seconds
B. Start	10 seconds
	Rest 60 seconds

DRILL #5- FULL BODY 1/4 TURNS

Explanation:

Two point stance, feet stationary; feet shoulder width apart; 1/4 turn right, return front. 1/4 turn left, return front; 1/4 turn left, return front. Repeat for required time.

A. Start   15 seconds

Rest 30 seconds

B. Start   15 seconds

The End

Variety keeps the athletes focused and interested. The worst scenario for a coach or athlete is that the workouts become mundane. We alternate some drills in our quick feet workout to keep the athletes thinking. Remember that this period is not a conditioning period, but a concentration of effort period. Always eliminate one drill for each added and keep rest intervals consistent. We alternate at Drills #3, #4, and #5; keeping Drills #1 and #2 consistent.

Every problem contains the seed of its own solution

DRILL #3 ALTERNATE

Equipment: Three dots one yard apart in an equilateral triangle.

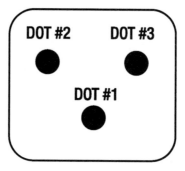

A. Start in good bent knee, flat back, head up position straddling Dot #1. Face straight ahead splitting the other two dots. The steps are right foot to Dot #2, left foot to Dot #2, right foot to Dot #3, left foot to Dot #1, right foot to Dot #1; then repeat immediately stepping with right foot first.

DURATION: 30 seconds; REST: one minute

Coaching Point: Always begin with right foot stepping first. The natural tendency will be to step with the left foot after the first cycle. Maintain good position and step – do not hop – the full distance to the dots. This point also applies to step B.

B. Same starting position as A. The steps are as follows: left foot to Dot #3, right foot to Dot #3, left foot to Dot #2, right foot to Dot #1, left foot to Dot #1, then repeat immediately with left foot stepping first.

DURATION: 30 seconds; REST: 1 minute

C. Same starting position on Dot #1, but with feet together. In this drill you hop the full distance to the dots on both feet. The hops are as follows: Dot #1 to Dot #2, back to Dot #1, to Dot #3 and back to Dot #1. Repeat rapidly.

DURATION: 30 seconds; REST: 1 minute

Coaching Point: Hop full distance to the dots and move as quickly as possible.

NOTE:

In all of these dot drills, emphasize concentration and full step speed. Focus on proper steps as per the drill and maintain good body position.

DRILL #4 ALTERNATE – JUMP ROPE FOR SPEED

Equipment: Jump rope

A. Both feet – Jump on both feet as rapidly as possible.	30 seconds
	Rest 1 minute
B. Right foot – Jump on right foot as rapidly as possible.	30 seconds
	Rest 1 minute
C. Left foot – Jump on left foot as rapidly as possible.	30 seconds
	Rest 1 minute

Coaching Point: Stress rapid jumps with immediate restart if the rope stops. Count jumps to gauge improvement.

DRILL #5 ALTERNATE – VOICE COMMAND MOVEMENT

Equipment: 6" step

Description: Athlete stands in good, bent knee, flat back position facing step. Coach chooses a jump word, such as SET. The goal of the athlete is to jump with both feet up onto the box and back down to a good position upon hearing the jump word. One jump every time the jump word is heard.

Coaching Point: Vary the way you say the jump word, soft, loud, in rapid succession or with pauses between. The coach can also call out words that rhyme with the jump word (if the jump word is SET, the commands can be bet, met, SET, let, get, SET, or any other variation).

Repeat three times for 30 seconds with one minute rest between sets.

GUIDELINES:

- Complete each drill rapidly and with total effort.
- Concentrate on speed.
- During rest periods, stretch or do nothing but concentrate on the next event.
- Follow the clock and don't get into a bull session during these drills. REMEMBER – THEY ARE BUILT AROUND YOUR CONCENTRATION. SO THINK. DON'T TALK!!

The largest room in the world is the room for improve-ment

6 PLYOMETRIC TRAINING

If the best things are not possible, make the best of things that are possible

Plyometric training is not a new mode of explosive training. Initial research began in the late 1960s in the Soviet Union and was furthered by other Eastern Block countries through the early 1970s. The Russians and East Germans have been successfully using plyometric training for sprinters for years. Plyometrics develop strength and power in the muscles involved in sprinting and jumping. Plyometric training bridges the gap between strength and power. All of us have seen the athlete who possesses superior strength yet cannot produce the necessary power to sprint a fast 40-yard dash. Plyometric training utilizes the myotics (stretch reflex), in the development of power by allowing the pre-stretching of the muscles in the amortization stage. Muscle will resist overstretching and the resulting kinetic energy will be utilized to cause a powerful contraction to prevent the overstretching of the muscle. The momentum generated by the athlete acts as the overload to eccentrically stretch the muscle before an immediate concentric contraction is initiated. The faster the transition from eccentric contraction to concentric contraction, the greater the overload in the concentric contraction will be. The following example will explain the theory of plyometrics. When a dropped basketball hits the floor, it is deformed and stores energy acquired in the drop. As the ball returns to its original shape, the stored kinetic energy is released and the ball returns to, or near, its drop height.

Muscles resist stretching by stimulating the stretch receptors, or muscle spindles, resulting in proprioceptive nerve impulses traveling to the spinal cord and returning to the same muscle. As a result, a powerful contraction occurs to prevent overstretching. This is the jump or hop. It is possible to exert as much as two times more tension during the explosive phase (if the muscle group has been pre-stretched and forced to break).

When you are rowing the boat, you don't have time to rock it

45

You may

be on top

of the

heap – but

remember

you are

still part

of it

To receive the full benefits of plyometric training, concentrate on performing all exercises in an explosive manner. Use proper form for each exercise and progress gradually. Plyometrics should only be practiced after a good strength base has been built.

GUIDELINES:

1. Complete only the plyometric exercises prescribed for your position. Consideration has been taken for physiological differences and specific position needs.

2. Always perform exercises on a padded or grass surface to avoid injury.

3. Each exercise should be a maximum effort and should be done with concentration on detail.

4. Each movement must be explosive to attain desired effects.

EXERCISE LIST

1. POWER SKIPS

Explanation: From the skipping position. Concentrate on drive off back leg, front leg high knee. Use arms to help height.

Exercise Goal: Height and hang time on each skip.

2. POWER JUMPS

Explanation: Feet shoulder width apart, back straight. Bend knees to 1/2 squat and explode upward, fully extending legs. Upon landing, repeat with no hesitation.

3. DEPTH JUMPING- 24" BOX

Explanation: Use two 24" boxes. Place the boxes four feet apart on a cushioned surface. Start on top of one box and face the other. Step (don't jump) off the box and land between the boxes. As you land, jump up onto the next box with an explosive motion.

Exercise Goal: It is imperative that as soon as you land on the ground, you explode up to the next box.

4. HORIZONTAL SPEED HOPS

Explanation: Off both legs, hop forward (as in a standing broad jump), land on both legs and immediately hop again.

Exercise Goal: SPEED IS THE GOAL. Cover the distance as rapidly as possible.

5. HORIZONTAL DISTANCE HOPS

Explanation: Off both legs, hop forward as far as possible (as in a standing broad jump), land and hop again as far as possible.

Exercise Goal: DISTANCE IS THE GOAL. Cover the required distance in as few hops as possible.

6. SPEED BOX JUMPS- 24" BOX

Explanation: Use one 24" box on the floor. Face the box, feet shoulder width apart. Explode up onto the box and immediately hop backwards off the box, then back up, and repeat.

Exercise Goal: Speed of movement through required repetitions. Continuous movement.

7. ONE LEG SPEED HOPS

Explanation: Start on one leg and hop as quickly as possible over required distance. Repeat with other leg.

Exercise Goal: Bend knee. Control balance and cover distance quickly.

8. BACKWARD DOUBLE LEG SPEED HOPS

Explanation: Off both legs. Hop for speed backwards. Cover distance as quickly as possible.

Exercise Goal: Maintain speed, balance and explosion while moving backwards rapidly.

9. LEAP STRIDE

Explanation: Exaggerate normal stride length by driving hard off back leg and over-reaching with front leg.

Exercise Goal: Continuous movement. Hard drive back leg. Cover distance in fewest leaps possible.

PLYOMETRIC EXERCISES

- During this cycle, plyometrics should be completed on Thursdays.
- Stretch prior to the plyometric workout.
- See Plyometric Exercise List for explanation of exercises.

OFFENSIVE AND DEFENSIVE LINE

1. *SPEED BOX JUMPS – 24" BOX* – three sets of 10 jumps (Rest one minute between sets)

2. *HORIZONTAL DISTANCE HOPS* – three sets of 20 yards (Rest 45 seconds between sets)

3. *HORIZONTAL SPEED HOPS* – three sets of 20 yards (Rest 45 seconds between sets)

4. *POWER JUMPS* – three sets of 10 jumps (Rest one minute between sets)

Noah did

not wait

for his

ship to

come in –

he built

one

TIGHT ENDS-LINEBACKERS

1. DEPTH JUMPS – 24" BOX – three sets 15 jumps (Rest one minute between sets)

2. HORIZONTAL DISTANCE HOPS – three sets 20 yards (Rest 45 seconds between sets)

3. HORIZONTAL SPEED HOPS – four sets 20 yards (Rest 45 seconds between sets)

4. POWER JUMPS – three sets 10 jumps (Rest one minute between sets)

WIDE RECEIVERS-DEFENSIVE BACKS-RUNNINGBACKS

1. DEPTH JUMPS – 24" BOX – four sets 15 jumps (Rest one minute between sets)

2. HORIZONTAL DISTANCE HOPS – four sets 20 yards (Rest 45 *seconds between sets)*

3. HORIZONTAL SPEED HOPS – four sets 20 yards (rest 45 seconds between sets)

4. POWER JUMPS – three sets 15 jumps (Rest one minute between sets)

Complete only the jumps prescribed and stick with the rest time allotments. As the cycle progresses, the overload will become greater as the season approaches. It is important that you stay on cycle to avoid burnout or overtraining. The cycle is designed to mesh with the other facets of your workout to achieve peak benefits.

7 STRENGTH TRAINING EXERCISES

Man's greatest moment: To be tested beyond what he thought might be his breaking point and succeed

In order to reap maximum benefits from your training, the exercises you perform must be executed with proper technique. The old adage "Practice does not make perfect, but perfect practice makes perfect" applies when training. Never sacrifice proper technique for more weight when lifting. Swinging, bouncing, arching and all other bad habits should be eliminated from your routine. Strict adherence to proper technique during your workouts will make you stronger and minimize the chance of injury. There is no text that can take the place of a partner when it comes to analyzing technical flaws in your workouts. Find a good partner and share constructive advice, using this text as your guide.

The world steps aside for the man who knows where he is going

BENCH PRESS

Muscles Affected: Pecs, deltoids, and triceps

Description: Lie on bench with back arched so that the shoulders and buttocks are touching the bench. Shoulder blades should be pulled tightly together. Feet should be firmly planted. Take a comfortable and firm overhand grip on the bar. Take lift-off from spotter and gain control of the bar. Lower the bar, under control, to the chest, just below the nipple line. Drive through the legs, keep the buttocks down, and push weight up and back at slight angle toward rack to lock out. Gain bar position control and repeat. Don't bounce the weight off the chest, and never raise the buttocks off of the bench. Always lock weight out. A good spotter is imperative in this exercise.

STRAIGHT BAR INCLINE PRESS

Muscles Affected: Upper pecs, deltoids, and triceps

Description: Grasp weight slightly wider than shoulder width. Keep the back flat and the feet planted. Take lift off from spotter and gain control of weight extended above upper chest. Lower weight, under control, to upper chest. Drive through the legs and push the weight straight up to start position. Maintain control throughout.

INCLINE DUMBBELL PRESS

Muscles Affected: Upper pecs, deltoids, and triceps

Description: Lie on bench with feet firmly planted. Begin with dumbbells positioned just under armpits in full stretched position. Maintain control of dumbbells as you push through legs to locked dumbbells together position. Pause at the top and return weight to full stretch starting position under control and repeat. Don't bounce the weight out of the armpit position, always maintain control. Use a spotter for safety.

MACHINE INCLINE PRESS

Muscles Affected: Upper pecs, deltoids, triceps

Description: Adjust seat so that the bar is even with the top of the shoulders. Grip is slightly wider than shoulder width. Keep feet planted and back tight against back pad. Push weight up to full extension and pause at the top. Lower weight under control to starting position. Pause and repeat.

TRICEP PUSH DOWN

Muscles Affected: Tricep

Description: Stand erect with one foot slightly forward. Take a close overhand grip on the bar, with the face in the center. Begin with bar just under nipples, keeping the elbows in tight and extending the arms down to lock out. Never jerk the weight down. Return the weight to the low chest starting position slowly and with control.

LYING TRICEP EXTENSION

Muscles Affected: Triceps

Description: With a close grip on the bar and the arms fully extended above the chest, keep the upper arms stationary and bend elbows to slowly lower the weight to the forehead. Keep the upper arms stationary and elbows up as you slowly return the weight to full extension. A spotter is recommended to lift weight on and off.

CLOSE GRIP LAT PULL

Muscles Affected: Lats and biceps

Description: From a close grip position with the arms fully extended and the head between the arms, pull the weight to the upper chest maintaining control. Return the weight to full extended position with the head in. Never let the weight jerk you, always maintain control.

WIDE GRIP LAT PULL

Muscles Affected: Lats and biceps

Description: Using an overhand grip slightly wider than shoulder width, begin the exercise with the arms fully extended and the head inside the arms. As you pull the weight down, move the head back. Touch the bar to the upper chest and then return the weight to the full extended position with control. Never let the weight jerk you, maintain control at all times.

EASY CURL

Muscles Affected: Biceps

Description: Stand erect, with the back straight and the weight fully extended. Curl weight from hanging position to just under the chin. Keep elbows tight to body and don't swing weight. Return weight, under control, to hang position.

HAMMER CURLS

Muscles Affected: Biceps and forearms

Description: Stand erect with dumbbells held straight down at sides of thighs. With the palms facing the body, curl one dumbbell up to shoulder height. Keep elbows in and maintain palms to body hand position. Work smoothly with no heaving. Alternate arms until required reps are performed.

MANUAL BACK NECK

Muscles Affected: Neck

Description: Sit in front of partner with the back straight. The partner places both hands on the back of the head. Move head through full range of motion. Begin with the chin on chest and smoothly raise head all the way back against partner's steady resistance. Make sure there are no jerky movements.

MANUAL FRONT NECK

Muscles Affected: Neck

Description: Sit in front of partner with back straight. The partner places both hands on forehead. Move head through full range of motion against partner's steady resistance. Pull the chin to the chest, then return to head back position with smooth motion.

MANUAL SIDE NECK

Muscles Affected: Neck

Description: Sit in front of a bench with the back straight. Partner places working hand on the side of head, just above the ear. His nonworking hand is on the opposite shoulder for support. Move the head through full range of motion, from side-to-side against partner's resistance. No jerking movements are to be made, and participants must be sure to move through full range of motion. Have partner switch hands to work other side of neck.

CRUNCHES

Muscles Affected: Abdominals

Description: Lie on the floor with the knees bent and the feet supported. Clasp hands behind the neck and raise the shoulders off the ground about six inches. Pause for a one count at the top and return slowly to the flat position. Don't jerk yourself up. Instead, maintain a slow steady rhythm throughout.

LEG UPS

Muscles Affected: Abdominals

Description: Lie flat with hands held palms down for support, raise the legs up and back until the buttocks and the lower back leave the floor. Pause at the top then return legs under control to the floor and repeat.

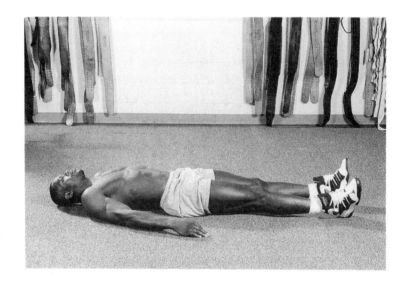

SEATED MILITARY PRESS

Muscles Affected: Deltoids, trapezius and triceps

Description: Grip the bar with an overhand grip slightly wider than shoulder width. Rack bar high on chest and make sure the back is kept straight. Drive through the legs and extend the bar to lock out position. Return the bar to the high chest rack position and repeat. If a seated military bench is not available, have your partner sit behind you, back straight, and use him for support (see photos).

SEATED MILITARY PRESS

Muscles Affected: Deltoids, trapezius, triceps

Description: Sit in machine so that the starting point of weight is at shoulder height. Feet should be firmly planted, back should be flat against pad with the head and eyes straight ahead. Drive through the legs and extend with the weight under control to lock out. Return weight to shoulder high position and repeat.

UPRIGHT ROW (HIGH PULL FROM HANG)

Muscles Affected: Deltoids, trapezius

Description: Hold bar with an overhand grip with the hands about ten inches apart. With the knees slightly bent, pull the weight up. Keep the weight close and under control all the way up to a chin high position with the elbows even with or higher than the bar. Return the weight to the starting point, maintaining control the entire time.

FRONT DELTOID RAISE

Muscles Affected: Anterior deltoids

Description: Hold the dumbbells at your sides with the palms facing in. Raise one dumbbell through the midline of the body to forehead height and return it to your side, maintaining control the entire distance. Alternate the arms, keeping arms straight and making sure to raise the dumbbells through the midline of the body.

SHRUG

Muscles Affected: Trapezius

Description: Stand erect with an overhand grip on the bar. Hands should be just outside of thighs. Keep the arms straight and pull the shoulders up toward the ears with control. Shrug the weight up as high as possible, then return the weight, under control, to starting full stretch position. Maintain erect position, don't bend forward when lowering the weight.

MANUAL SHOULDERS

Muscles Affected: Anterior deltoids

Description: From an extended arm full stretch position, raise arms straight ahead, against the resistance of a partner, to the height of your forehead. Hold arms up and then resist partner's pressure back to the starting point. Make sure to start each repetition with the arms stretched past the hips.

MANUAL SHOULDERS

Muscles Affected: Medial deltoids

Description: With the arms extended in front of the body, move them out and to the side against your partner's resistance. Finish at eye height and then resist partner's pressure back to the starting point. Try to maintain straight arm position throughout.

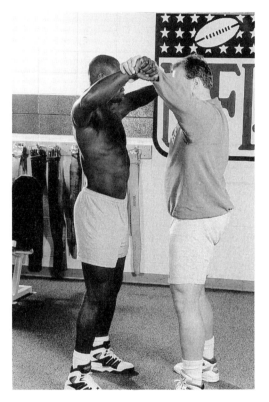

HIGH PULL FROM FLOOR

Muscles Affected: Glutes, quadriceps, hamstrings, hips, and lower back

Description: With feet shoulder width apart, the bar should start resting against the shins. Extend the arms and grasp the bar in an overhand grip. Squat so that the arms remain extended and the back is flat, with the head up and chest out. The beginning portion of the lift is steady, not jerky. Maintain the flat back position and gain momentum with the bar. When the bar reaches a point just above the knee caps, you should try to literally jump straight up through the roof with the weight. This action forces the hips through, which creates an acceleration that raises the bar sternum high. Allow the weight to return to the waist, then the floor. Return to your original position and repeat.

SQUAT

Muscles Affected: Glutes, quadriceps, hamstrings, lower back, and hips

Description: Rack bar comfortably on back (some prefer high rack, some low). Feet should be slightly wider than shoulder width apart with the toes pointed slightly out. Your back must remain flat through entire lift. Descend, maintaining control, to a position with the upper thigh approximately two inches above parallel. On the upward motion, the head should be straight with the eyes looking up as you accelerate the weight up. Slow down just before full leg extension and maintain your balance. Focus on descending control, and then upward acceleration.

LEG PRESS

Muscles Affected: Quadriceps, hamstrings, and glutes

Description: Place feet in a comfortable position, about shoulder width apart. Bring weight down, maintaining control, until the thighs touch the chest. Accelerate the weight up to a position just short of lock out then slow down. Never hyperextend knees at the top. Down stroke maintain control, accelerate on up stroke. For multiple sets, vary the foot position.

LEG EXTENSION

Muscles Affected: Quadriceps

Description: Sit on leg extension machine with the knee joint just over the edge of the bench. Hold the seat hard, keep buttocks down, and extend legs to full extension while maintaining control. Return to the full bent position.

LEG CURL

Muscles Affected: Hamstrings

Description: Lie on the leg curl machine with the knee caps just off the bench edge. Keep hips down and curl the weight to the buttocks, maintaining control. Return the weight, maintaining control, to full extension.

DUMBBELL FRONT LUNGE

Muscles Affected: Quadriceps, hamstrings, and glutes

Description: Stand erect with the dumbbells at your side, and with the feet shoulder width apart. Take a long step forward, keep your back straight and bend one leg until your thigh is parallel to the floor. Push back to the starting position and repeat.

STANDING CALF RAISE

Muscles Affected: Calves

Description: With the feet together, stand with the balls of your feet on the platform. From a full stretched position, extend up as high as possible, pause, and then return slowly to the full stretched position, pause, repeat. When performing multiple sets, vary toe position (toes in, toes out) for maximum effect.

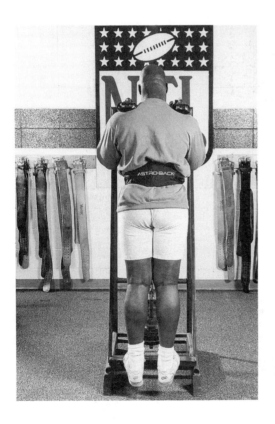 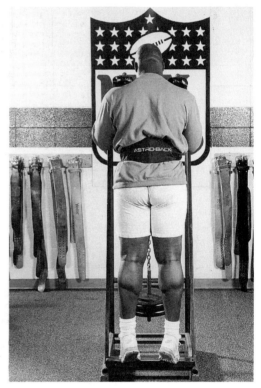

CALF RAISE ON LEG PRESS

Muscles Affected: Calves

Description: Feet together, place balls of the feet on the bottom of the leg press. From a full stretched position, extend the weight under control as high as possible and pause at the top. Return the weight slowly to a full stretch position, pause, and repeat. When performing multiple sets, vary toe position (toes in, toes out) for maximum effect.

STRAIGHT LEG DEAD LIFT FROM SIX INCH BOX

Muscles Affected: Lower back, glutes and hamstrings

Description: Stand on a six inch box with slightly bent knees. Grasp bar with overhand grip slightly wider than shoulder width apart. Slowly stand erect, keeping the bar close to the body. When erect, return slowly to full starting position allowing weight to pause on the floor briefly before beginning next step.

HYPEREXTENSION

Muscles Affected: Lower back, glutes, hamstrings

Hands clasped behind the head. From a full down stretched position, slowly raise the body to full extension. Do not hyper extend the back. When body is straight, return with the body under control to the full stretched position.

8 THE PROGRAM

If something goes wrong, it is more important to decide who is going to fix it than who is to blame

We take a holistic approach to our weight training program. Our major goal is to develop stronger, faster, quicker and more explosive athletes. Preparing athletes to endure an entire football season, at any level, requires a multifaceted approach.

A weight training program should be designed to mesh with the other components of the conditioning program, to provide athletes with a total program that trains all the links to success. Increasing power through the full range of motion not only makes an athlete more effective in his performance, it reduces his risk of becoming injured. If an injury does occur, as is bound to happen on occasion, a holistically trained athlete will return to action faster.

Equipment limitations, time restrictions and coaching availability might make it difficult to implement all of the components of a total conditioning program. The following should be studied and used, either in total or in part to strengthen an existing program. As athletes progress to higher levels of play, a total conditioning program becomes more and more vital.

The Weight Training Program outlined here is designed with cycles that maintain a progressive overload to a peaking process. The cycles are set up to allow consideration to other demands of the conditioning program (running, plyometrics, speed improvement drills). The program is oriented to provide the necessary power development to improve the key elements of speed and explosion.

Follow the program as it is and remember to work each muscle group thoroughly with intensity on its prescribed day. The lifting days are Monday, Tuesday, Thursday and Friday.

Weight training is an anaerobic activity and promotes the same conditioning qualities that football requires.

The chief

duty of a

man is

to master

life, not

endure it

Each repetition in the broad range movements (squat, high pulls, bench press, leg press and dead lift) should be completed with maximum acceleration on each repetition. This is the most effective type of training for developing explosive power.

The theory of Compensatory Acceleration states that more muscle fiber is forced to fire on each repetition when total effort is expelled to accelerate the weight as rapidly as possible. For example, during a set of squats where you are doing eight repetitions, the first four reps are relatively easy. Only on the last four do you really expend much effort. According to the Compensatory Acceleration theory, if on each repetition of that set of eight you explode up with the weight, accelerating it as quickly as possible, you force each rep to become more difficult, thereby receiving maximum benefit and more muscle recruitment. Rapidly accelerating the weight on each repetition also develops the neuromuscular pathways that explosive power requires. Remember, broad range movements (squat, high pulls, bench press, leg press and dead lift) are best suited to this type of training. Application of the theory would be of little value during small range movements such as the bicep curl.

Do not neglect any of the components of the program. The program is designed to cover every aspect of your off-season conditioning.

On the following pages, you will find all of the workouts listed day-by-day with the corresponding cycles for each workout. Simply use the percentage chart provided to plug in your personal numbers.

MONDAY (HEAVY DAY)

ABDOMINALS. CHEST. TRICEPS. BACK, BICEPS AND NECK

STRETCH - 10 MINUTES

ABDOMINALS

CRUNCHES	4 sets of 30 reps
LEG UPS	4 sets of 25 reps

CHEST

BENCH	Refer to bench cycle on next page
INCLINE	Medium Heavy - 6-8 reps
	Heavy - 6 reps
	Heavy - 6 reps
	Heavy - 6 reps

TRICEPS

TRICEP EXTENSION	Heavy - 6-8 reps
or	Heavy - 6-8 reps
PUSH DOWN	Heavy - 6-8 reps
or	Heavy - 6-8 reps
CLOSE GRIP BENCH	
or	
WEIGHTED DIPS	

LATS

LAT PULLS	Medium Heavy - 10 reps
(Close Grip)	Heavy - 6-8 reps
(Pull to chest)	Heavy - 6-8 reps
LAT PULLS	Heavy - 6-8 reps
(Wide Grip)	Heavy - 6-8 reps
(Pull to chest)	Heavy - 6-8 reps
1 ARM BENT ROW	Heavy - 8 reps
(Each arm)	Heavy - 8 reps

BICEPS

CURLS	Medium Heavy - 6-8 reps
(Straight Bar)	Heavy - 6-8 reps
or	Heavy - 6-8 reps
(Easy Curl)	Heavy - 6-8 reps
HAMMER CURLS	Heavy - 8 reps
(Dumbbells)	Heavy - 8 reps
	Heavy - 8 reps

NECK

NECK MACHINE	4 ways x 10 reps
or	4 ways x 10 reps
MANUAL NECK	4 ways x 10 reps
(All four directions)	4 ways x 10 reps

STRETCH - 10 MINUTES

BENCH PRESS CYCLE #1 —

GOAL: 12 WEEK CYCLE TO TEST FOR MAX

WEEK #1

Monday

50% of Max x 10 reps
60% of Max x 4 sets of 8 reps
50% of Max x Max reps

Thursday

50% of Max x 10 reps
60% of Max x 4 sets of 8 reps
50% of Max x Max reps

WEEK #2

Monday

50% of Max x 10 reps
60% of Max x 2 sets of 8 reps
65% of Max x 2 sets of 8 reps
60% of Max x Max reps

Thursday

50% of Max x 10 reps
65% of Max x 8 reps
70% of Max x 3 sets of 6 reps
65% of Max x Max reps

If you are able to complete all the required reps in a workout for two workouts in a row, then you should move up to the next highest Max on the percentage chart (see the end of the chapter). Conversely, if you fail to complete all required repetitions for two workouts in a row, then adjust your Max down. This procedure should be followed throughout this entire cycle.

WEEK #3

Monday

60% of Max x 8 reps
75% of Max x 6 reps
80% of Max x 4 sets of 5 reps
75% of Max x 5 reps (PAUSE)

Thursday

60% of Max x 8 reps
75% of Max x 6 reps
80% of Max x 2 sets of 5 reps
75% of Max x 5 reps (PAUSE)
75% of Max x 5 reps (PAUSE)

WEEK #4

Monday

60% of Max x 8 reps
75% of Max x 6 reps
80% of Max x 4 sets of 5 reps
75% of Max x 5 reps (PAUSE)

Thursday

60% of Max x 8 reps
75% of Max x 6 reps
80% of Max x 2 sets of 5 reps
75% of Max x 5 reps (PAUSE)
75% of Max x 5 reps (PAUSE)

WEEK #5

Monday

60% of Max x 8 reps
75% of Max x 6 reps
80% of Max x 3 sets of 5 reps
75% of Max x 5 reps (PAUSE)
75% of Max x 5 reps (PAUSE)

Thursday

60% of Max x 8 reps

75% of Max x 6 reps

80% of Max x 2 sets of 5 reps

75% of Max x 5 reps (PAUSE)

75% of Max x 5 reps (PAUSE)

(Make sure to reevaluate your Max constantly.)

WEEK #6

Monday

60% of Max x 8 reps

75% of Max x 6 reps

80% of Max x 3 sets of 5 reps

75% of Max x 5 reps (PAUSE)

75% of Max x 5 reps (PAUSE)

Thursday

60% of Max x 8 reps

75% of Max x 6 reps

80% of Max x 2 sets of 5 reps

75% of Max x 5 reps

75% of Max x Max reps (PAUSE)

WEEK #7

Monday

60% of Max x 8 reps

75% of Max x 6 reps

80% of Max x 5 reps

85% of Max x 3 sets of 4 reps

75% of Max x Max reps (PAUSE)

Thursday

60% of Max x 8 reps

75% of Max x 6 reps

80% of Max x 5 reps

85% of Max x 2 sets of 4 reps

75% of Max x Max reps (PAUSE)

WEEK #8

Monday

60% of Max x 8 reps

75% of Max x 6 reps

80% of Max x 5 reps

85% of Max x 4 sets of 4 reps

Thursday

60% of Max x 8 reps

75% of Max x 6 reps

80% of Max x 5 reps

85% of Max x 2 sets of 4 reps

80% of Max x Max reps (PAUSE)

WEEK #9

Monday

60% of Max x 8 reps

75% of Max x 6 reps

80% of Max x 5 reps

85% of Max x 4 set of 4 reps

Thursday

60% of Max x 8 reps

75% of Max x 6 reps

80% of Max x 5 reps

85% of Max x 2 sets of 4 reps

80% of Max x Max reps (PAUSE)

WEEK #10

Monday

60% of Max x 8 reps

75% of Max x 6 reps

85% of Max x 4 reps

90% of Max x 2 sets of 3 reps

80% of Max x Max reps (PAUSE)

Thursday

60% of Max x 8 reps

75% of Max x 6 reps

85% of Max x 4 reps

90% of Max x 3 reps

80% of Max x Max reps (PAUSE)

WEEK #11

Monday

60% of Max x 8 reps
75% of Max x 6 reps
85% of Max x 4 reps
90% of Max x 3 reps
92% of Max x 2 reps
80% of Max x Max reps (PAUSE)
80% of Max x Max reps

Thursday

60% of Max x 8 reps
75% of Max x 6 reps
85% of Max x 4 reps
90% of Max x 2 sets of 3 reps
80% of Max x Max reps (PAUSE)

WEEK #12

Monday (Last bench before testing)

60% of Max x 8 reps
75% of Max x 6 reps
85% of Max x 4 reps
90% of Max x 1 repetition
95% of Max x 1 repetition
80% of Max x Max reps (PAUSE)

TUESDAY (HEAVY DAY)
SHOULDERS, LEGS AND LOW BACK

STRETCH - 10 MINUTES

SHOULDERS

HIGH PULL FROM HANG	Medium Heavy - 8 reps	
(Explosive Upright Row)	Heavy - 6-8 reps	
	Heavy - 6-8 reps	
	Heavy - 6-8 reps	
	Heavy - 6-8 reps	
FRONT DELTOID RAISES	Heavy - 6-8 reps	
	Heavy - 6-8 reps	
	Heavy - 6-8 reps	
MANUAL SHOULDER	Front & Side - 8 reps	
	Front & Side - 8 reps	
	Front & Side - 8 reps	
SHRUGS	Heavy - 8 reps	
	Heavy - 8 reps	
	Heavy - 8 reps	
	Heavy - 8 reps	
	Heavy - 8 reps	

LEGS

*SQUATS	Refer to squat cycle on next page	
(2 inches above parallel)		
LEG PRESS	Heavy - 8 reps	
	Heavy - 8 reps	
	Heavy - 8 reps	
LEG EXTENSION	Heavy - 8 reps	
	Heavy - 8 reps	
	Heavy - 8 reps	
	Heavy - 8 reps	
LEG CURL	Heavy - 8 reps	
	Heavy - 8 reps	
	Heavy - 8 reps	
	Heavy - 8 reps	
CALF RAISE	Medium x 20 reps	
(Slow Full Range)	Medium x 20 reps	
	Medium x 20 reps	

LOW BACK

HYPEREXTENSION	4 sets x 20 reps

STRETCH - 10 MINUTES

* If, for medical reasons, you are unable to squat, the cycle should then be followed on the leg press

SQUAT CYCLE #1
GOAL: 12 WEEK CYCLE TO TEST FOR MAX

WEEK #1

Tuesday
50% of Max x 8 reps
65% of Max x 8 reps
70% of Max x 3 sets of 8 reps

If you are able to complete all required repetitions in the workout for 2 workouts in a row, then you should move up to a higher max on the percentage chart. Conversely, if you fail to complete all required repetitions for 2 workouts in a row, you should adjust your max down. This procedure should be followed throughout this entire cycle. (Constantly evaluate yourself.)

WEEK #2

Tuesday
50% of Max x 8 reps
65% of Max x 8 reps
75% of Max x 5 reps
80% of Max x 3 sets of 5 reps
70% of Max x 8 reps

WEEK #3

Tuesday
50% of Max x 8 reps
65% of Max x 6 reps
75% of Max x 5 reps
80% of Max x 3 sets of 5 reps
75% of Max x 8 reps

WEEK #4

Tuesday
50% of Max x 8 reps
65% of Max x 6 reps
75% of Max x 5 reps
80% of Max x 3 sets of 5 reps
75% of Max x 5 reps

WEEK #5

Tuesday
50% of Max x 8 reps
65% of Max x 6 reps
75% of Max x 5 reps
85% of Max x 3 sets of 5 reps
80% of Max x 5 reps

WEEK #6

Tuesday
50% of Max x 8 reps
65% of Max x 5 reps
75% of Max x 5 reps
85% of Max x 3 reps
80% of Max x 5 reps

WEEK #7

Tuesday
50% of Max x 8 reps
65% of Max x 5 reps
75% of Max x 5 reps
85% of Max x 5 reps
90% of Max x 2 sets of 3 reps
80% of Max x 5 reps

WEEK #8

Tuesday
50% of Max x 8 reps
65% of Max x 5 reps
75% of Max x 5 reps
85% of Max x 5 reps
90% of Max x 2 sets of 3 reps
80% of Max x 5 reps

WEEK #9

Tuesday
50% of Max x 8 reps
65% of Max x 5 reps
75% of Max x 5 reps
85% of Max x 4 reps
90% of Max x 3 reps
92% of Max x 2 reps
80% of Max x 5 reps

WEEK #10

Tuesday
50% of Max x 8 reps
65% of Max x 5 reps
75% of Max x 5 reps
85% of Max x 4 reps
90% of Max x 3 reps
92% of Max x 2 reps
80% of Max x 5 reps

WEEK #11

Tuesday *(Last squat day before testing)*
50% of Max x 8 reps
65% of Max x 5 reps
75% of Max x 4 reps
85% of Max x 3 reps
90% of Max x 1 rep
95% of Max x 1 rep
80% of Max x 5 reps

WEDNESDAY — OFF DAY

THURSDAY

CHEST, TRICEPS, BACK, BICEPS, ABDOMINALS AND NECK

STRETCH - 10 MINUTES

CHEST

BENCH	(Refer to bench cycle)
INCLINE	Heavy - 8 reps
	Heavy - 8 reps
	Heavy - 8 reps

TRICEPS

LYING TRICEP EXTENSION	Heavy - 8 reps
or	
TRICEP PUSH DOWN	Heavy - 8 reps
or	Heavy - 8 reps
WEIGHTED DIPS	Heavy - Max reps to failure

LATS

LAT PULLS	
(Close Grip)	Medium Heavy - 8 reps
(Pull to Chest)	Heavy - 8-10 reps
	Heavy - 8-10 reps
	Heavy - 8-10 reps
LAT PULLS	
(Wide Grip)	Heavy - 8-10 reps
(Pull to Chest)	Heavy - 8-10 reps
	Heavy - 8-10 reps
	Heavy - 8-10 reps

BICEPS

CURLS	Medium Heavy - 10 reps
(Straight Bar)	Heavy - 8-10 reps
or	Heavy - 8-10 reps
(Easy Curl)	Heavy - 8-10 reps
HAMMER CURLS	Heavy - 8-10 reps
or	Heavy - 8-10 reps
MANUAL CURLS	Heavy - 8-10 reps (Superset)

ABDOMINALS

SUPERSET (No Rest)	Crunch x 30 reps
	Leg up x 25 reps
	Crunch x 30 reps
	Leg up x 25 reps
	Crunch x 30 reps
	Leg up x 25 reps

NECK

NECK MACHINE	4 ways x 10 reps
or	4 ways x 10 reps
MANUAL NECK	4 ways x 10 reps
(All Four Directions)	4 ways x 10 reps

STRETCH - 10 MINUTES

FRIDAY

LOWER BACK, SHOULDERS, LEGS

STRETCH - 10 MINUTES

ERECTORS/LOWER BACK/LEGS/HIPS

	HIGH PULL (from floor)	Light - 8 reps
		Medium/Heavy - 8 reps
		Heavy - 5 reps
		Heavy - 5 reps
		Heavy - 5 reps

SHOULDERS

	SEATED MILITARY PRESS	Medium - 8 reps
		Heavy - 8 reps
		Heavy - 8 reps
		Heavy - 8 reps
		Heavy - 8 reps
	FRONT DELTOID RAISES	Heavy - 8 reps
		Heavy - 8 reps
		Heavy - 8 reps
	MANUAL SHOULDER	Front & Side - 8 reps
		Front & Side - 8 reps
	SHRUGS	Medium - 15 reps
		Medium - 15 reps
		Medium - 15 reps
		Medium - 15 reps

LEGS

	SQUATS	50% of Max x 20 reps
	High Rep; 3/4 depth	60% of Max x 20 reps
	(3 inch above parallel)	65% of Max x 20 reps
	REST 4 MINUTES	
	SUPERSET (No rest between sets)	
	Leg Press	Heavy - 8 reps
	Leg Extension	Medium - 15 reps
	Leg Press	Heavy - 8 reps
	Leg Extension	Medium - 15 reps
	Leg Press	Heavy - 8 reps
	Leg Extension	Medium - 15 reps
	Leg Press	Heavy - 8 reps
	Leg Extension	Medium - 15 reps
	REST 4 MINUTES	
	SUPERSET (No rest between sets)	
	Dumbbell Lunge	Medium/Heavy - 8 reps (each leg)
	Leg Curl	Heavy - 8 reps
	Calf Raise	Heavy - 15 reps
	Dumbbell Lunge	Medium/Heavy - 8 reps (each leg)
	Leg Curl	Heavy - 8 reps
	Calf Raise	Heavy - 15 reps
	REST 3 MINUTES	
	SUPERSET (No rest between sets)	
	Straight Leg Dead Lift	Light - 10 reps
	Hyperextensions	- 15 reps
	Straight Leg Dead Lift	Light - 10 reps
	Hyperextensions	- 15 reps
	Straight Leg Dead Lift	Light - 10 reps
	Hyperextensions	- 15 reps

STRETCH - 10 MINUTES

PERCENTAGE CHART

max. weight	55%	60%	65%	70%	75%	80%	85%	90%	92%	95%
200	110	120	130	140	150	160	170	180	184	190
205	113	123	133	143	154	164	174	184	189	195
210	115	126	136	147	158	168	178	189	193	199
215	118	129	140	150	161	172	183	193	198	204
220	121	132	143	154	165	176	187	198	202	209
225	124	135	146	157	169	180	191	202	207	214
230	126	138	149	161	173	184	195	207	212	218
235	129	141	153	164	176	188	200	211	216	223
240	132	144	156	168	180	192	204	216	221	228
245	135	147	159	171	184	196	208	220	225	233
250	137	150	162	175	188	200	212	225	230	237
255	140	153	166	178	191	204	217	229	235	242
260	143	156	169	182	195	208	221	234	239	247
265	146	159	172	185	199	212	225	238	244	252
270	148	162	175	189	203	216	229	243	248	256
275	151	165	179	192	206	220	234	247	253	261
280	154	168	182	196	210	224	238	252	258	266
285	157	171	185	199	214	228	242	256	262	271
290	159	174	188	203	218	232	246	261	267	275
295	162	177	192	206	221	236	251	265	271	280
300	165	180	195	210	225	240	255	270	276	285
305	168	183	198	213	229	244	259	274	281	290
310	170	186	201	217	233	248	263	279	285	294
315	173	189	205	220	236	252	268	283	290	299
320	176	192	208	224	240	256	272	288	294	304
325	179	195	211	227	244	260	276	292	299	309
330	181	198	214	231	248	264	280	297	304	313
335	184	201	218	234	251	268	285	301	308	318
340	187	204	221	238	255	272	289	306	313	323
345	190	207	224	241	259	276	293	310	317	328
350	192	210	227	245	263	280	297	315	322	332
355	195	213	231	248	266	284	302	324	327	337
360	198	216	234	252	270	288	306	328	331	342

max. weight	55%	60%	65%	70%	75%	80%	85%	90%	92%	95%
365	201	219	237	255	274	292	310	333	336	347
370	203	222	240	259	278	296	314	337	340	351
375	206	225	244	262	281	300	319	342	345	356
380	209	228	247	266	285	304	323	346	350	361
385	212	231	250	269	289	308	327	351	354	366
390	214	234	253	273	293	312	331	355	359	370
395	217	237	257	276	296	316	336	360	363	375
400	220	240	260	280	300	320	340	364	368	380
405	223	243	263	283	304	324	344	369	373	385
410	225	246	266	287	308	328	348	373	377	389
415	228	249	270	290	311	332	353	378	382	394
420	231	252	273	294	315	336	357	382	386	399
425	234	255	276	297	319	340	361	387	291	404
430	236	258	279	301	323	344	365	391	396	408
435	239	261	283	304	326	348	370	396	400	413
440	242	264	286	308	330	353	374	400	405	418
445	245	267	289	311	334	356	378	405	409	423
450	247	270	292	315	338	360	382	409	414	427
455	250	273	296	318	341	364	387	414	419	432
460	253	276	299	322	345	368	391	419	423	437
465	256	279	302	325	349	372	395	423	428	442
470	258	282	305	329	353	376	399	427	432	446
475	261	285	309	332	356	380	404	432	437	451
480	264	288	312	336	360	384	408	436	442	456
485	267	291	315	339	364	388	412	441	446	461
490	269	294	318	343	368	392	416	445	451	465
495	272	297	322	346	371	396	421	450	455	470
500	275	300	325	350	375	400	425	454	460	475
505	278	303	328	353	379	404	429	459	465	480
510	280	306	331	357	383	408	433	463	469	484
515	283	309	335	360	386	412	438	468	474	489
520	286	312	338	364	390	416	442	472	478	494
525	289	315	341	367	394	420	446	477	483	499
530	291	318	344	371	398	424	450	481	488	503

max. weight	55%	60%	65%	70%	75%	80%	85%	90%	92%	95%
540	297	324	351	378	405	432	459	486	497	513
545	300	327	354	381	409	436	463	490	501	518
550	302	330	357	385	413	440	467	495	506	522
555	305	333	361	388	416	444	472	499	511	527
560	308	336	364	392	420	448	476	504	515	532
565	311	339	367	395	424	452	480	508	520	537
570	313	342	370	399	428	456	484	513	524	541
575	316	345	374	402	431	460	489	517	529	546
580	319	348	377	406	435	464	493	522	534	551
585	322	351	380	409	439	468	197	526	538	556
590	324	354	383	413	443	472	501	531	543	560
595	327	357	387	416	446	476	506	535	547	565
600	330	360	390	420	450	480	510	540	552	570
605	333	363	393	423	454	484	514	544	557	575
610	335	366	396	427	458	488	518	549	561	579
615	338	369	400	430	461	492	523	553	566	584
620	341	372	403	434	465	496	527	558	570	589
625	344	375	406	437	469	500	531	562	575	594
630	346	378	409	441	473	504	535	567	580	598
635	349	381	413	444	476	508	540	571	584	603
640	352	384	416	448	480	512	544	576	589	608
645	355	387	419	451	484	516	548	580	593	613
650	357	390	422	455	488	520	552	585	598	617
655	360	393	426	458	491	524	557	589	603	622
660	363	396	429	462	495	528	561	594	607	627
665	366	399	432	465	499	532	565	598	612	632
670	368	402	435	469	503	536	569	603	616	636
675	371	405	439	472	506	540	574	607	621	641
680	374	408	442	476	510	544	578	612	626	646
685	377	411	445	479	514	548	582	616	630	651
690	379	414	448	483	518	552	586	621	635	655
695	382	417	452	486	521	556	591	625	639	660
700	385	420	455	490	525	560	595	630	644	665
705	388	423	458	493	529	564	599	634	649	670

max. weight	55%	60%	65%	70%	75%	80%	85%	90%	92%	95%
710	390	426	461	497	533	568	603	639	653	674
715	393	429	465	500	536	572	608	643	658	679
720	396	432	468	504	540	576	612	648	662	684
725	399	435	471	507	544	580	616	652	667	689
730	401	438	474	511	548	584	620	657	672	693
735	404	441	478	514	551	588	625	661	676	698
740	407	444	481	518	555	592	629	666	681	703
745	410	447	484	521	559	296	633	670	685	708
750	412	450	487	525	563	600	637	675	690	712
755	415	453	491	528	566	604	642	679	695	717
760	418	456	494	532	570	608	646	684	699	722
765	421	459	497	535	574	612	650	688	704	727
770	423	462	500	539	578	616	654	693	708	731
775	426	465	504	542	581	620	659	697	713	736
780	429	468	507	546	585	624	663	702	718	741
785	432	471	510	549	589	628	667	706	722	746
790	434	474	513	553	593	632	671	711	727	750
795	437	477	517	556	596	636	676	715	731	755
800	440	480	520	560	600	640	680	720	736	760
805	443	183	523	563	604	644	684	724	741	765
810	445	486	526	567	608	648	688	729	745	769
815	448	489	530	570	611	652	693	733	750	774
820	451	492	533	574	615	656	697	738	754	779
825	454	495	536	577	619	660	701	742	759	784
830	456	498	539	581	623	664	705	747	764	788
835	459	501	543	584	626	668	710	751	768	793
840	462	504	546	588	630	672	714	756	773	798
845	465	507	549	591	634	676	718	760	777	803
850	467	510	552	595	638	680	722	765	782	807

9 THE DAILY OFF-SEASON SCHEDULE

When you call on a thoroughbred, he gives you all the speed, heart and desire in him. When you call on a jackass, all he does is squawk and kick

This is the daily off-season schedule that I recommend for my players. Simply look at the day's activities and turn to the corresponding section (i.e. weight program, plyometrics, fast feet and timing) for details.

WEEK ONE

Monday
    Stretch
    Weights
    Stretch

Tuesday
    Stretch
    Weights
    Stretch

Wednesday
    Stretch
    Fast Feet Timing Drills
    Stretch

Thursday
    Stretch
    Weights
    Stretch

Friday
    Stretch
    Fast Feet Timing Drills
    Weights
    Stretch

Saturday
    Stretch
    Active Rest

Sunday
    OFF DAY

WEEK TWO

Monday
  Stretch
  Fast Feet Timing Drills
  Weights
  Stretch

Tuesday
  Stretch
  Weights
  Stretch

Wednesday
  Stretch
  Fast Feet Timing Drills
  Stretch

Thursday
  Stretch
  Weights
  Stretch

Friday
  Stretch
  Fast Feet Timing Drills
  Weights
  Stretch

Saturday
  Stretch
  Active Rest

Sunday
  OFF DAY

WEEK THREE

Monday
  Stretch
  Fast Feet Timing Drills
  Weights
  Stretch

Tuesday
  Stretch
  Weights
  Stretch

Wednesday
  Stretch
  Fast Feet Timing Drills
  Bike: Sprint 30 seconds, easy one
    minute, repeat 10 working reps.
  Stretch

Thursday
  Stretch
  Weights
  Stretch

Friday
  Stretch
  Fast Feet Timing Drills
  Bike or StairMaster - 20 minutes;
    Medium resistance
  Weights
  Stretch

Saturday
  Stretch
  Active Rest

Sunday
  OFF DAY

WEEK FOUR

Monday
Stretch
Fast Feet Timing Drills
Weights
Jump Rope: All positions (8 min-
    utes, 1 minute work, 1 minute rest,
    continued for 8 minutes working)
Stretch

Tuesday
Stretch
Weights
Stretch

Wednesday
Stretch
Fast Feet Timing Drills
Bike: Sprint 30 seconds, easy one
    minute, repeat 10 working reps.
Stretch

Thursday
Stretch
Weights
Stretch

Friday
Stretch
Fast Feet Timing Drills
Bike or StairMaster - 20 minutes;
    Medium resistance
Weights
Stretch

Saturday
Active Rest

Sunday
OFF DAY

WEEK FIVE

Monday
Stretch
Fast Feet Timing Drills
Weights
Jump Rope:
OL, DL — 10 minutes
TE, LB, QB — 11 minutes
WR, RB, DB — 12 minutes
Stretch

Tuesday
Stretch
Weights
Stretch

Wednesday
Stretch
Fast Feet Timing Drills
Stretch
Bike: Sprint 30 seconds, easy one
    minute, repeat 12 working reps.

Thursday
Stretch
Weights
Stretch

Friday
Stretch
Fast Feet Timing Drills
Bike or StairMaster - 20 minutes,
    Medium resistance
Weights
Stretch

Saturday
Active Rest

Sunday
OFF DAY

WEEK SIX

Monday

Stretch
Fast Feet Timing Drills
Weights
Jump Rope:
OL, DL — 10 minutes
TE, LB, QB — 11 minutes
WR, RB, DB —12 minutes

Tuesday

Stretch
Weights
Stretch

Wednesday

Stretch
Fast Feet Timing Drills
Stretch
Bike: Sprint 30 seconds, easy one
  minute, repeat 12 working reps

Thursday

Stretch
Weights
Stretch

Friday

Stretch
Fast Feet Timing Drills
Bike or StairMaster – 20 minutes;
  Medium resistance
Weights
Stretch

Saturday

Active Rest

Sunday

OFF DAY

WEEK SEVEN

Monday

Stretch
Fast Feet Timing Drills
All Positions: 12 x 100 yards -
  Continuous movement, comfort-
  able stride pace. Every 200 yards
  do 10 push-ups

Tuesday

Stretch
Weights
Stretch

Wednesday

Stretch
Fast Feet Timing Drills
All Positions: Jog 40 seconds, sprint
  10 seconds, repeat for 10 sprints
  with 40-second jogs in-between
  (continuous movement)
Stretch

Thursday

Stretch
Weights
Plyometrics
Stretch

Friday

Stretch
Fast Feet Timing Drills
Timed Run:
OL, DL — 14 minutes
TE, LB, QB — 16 minutes
WR, RB, DB — 18 minutes

Saturday

Active Rest

Sunday

OFF DAY

WEEK EIGHT

Monday
Stretch
Fast Feet Timing Drills
All Positions: 12 x 100 yards -
  Continuous movement, comfort-
  able stride pace. Every 200 yards,
  10 push ups

Tuesday
Stretch
Weights
Stretch

Wednesday
Stretch
Fast Feet Timing Drills
OL, DL - Jog 40 seconds, sprint
  10 seconds, repeat 10 times,
  continuous movement
TE, LB, QB - Jog 40 seconds, sprint
  10 seconds, repeat 12 times,
  continuous movement
WR, RB, DB - Jog 40 seconds,
  sprint 10 seconds, repeat 14 times,
  continuous movement

Thursday
Stretch
Weights
Plyometrics
Stretch

Friday
Stretch
Fast Feet Timing Drills
Timed Run:
OL, DL — 16 minutes
TE, LB, QB — 18 minutes
WR, RB, DB — 20 minutes
Weights
Stretch

Saturday   Active Rest
Sunday   OFF DAY

WEEK NINE

Monday
Stretch
Fast Feet Timing Drills
All Positions - 12 x 100
  yards - Continuous movement,
  comfortable stride pace. Every 200
  yards, 10 push ups

Tuesday
Stretch
Weights
Stretch

Wednesday
Stretch
Fast Feet Timing Drills
OL, DL - Jog 40 seconds, sprint 10
  seconds, repeat 10 times, continuous movement
TE, LB, QB - Jog 40 seconds,
  sprint 10 seconds, repeat 12 times,
  continuous movement
WR, RB, DB - Jog 40 seconds,
  sprint 10 seconds, repeat 14 times,
  continuous movement

Thursday
Stretch
Weights
Plyometrics
Stretch

Friday
Stretch
Fast Feet Timing Drills
Timed Run:
OL, DL — 16 minutes
TE, LB, QB — 18 minutes
WR, RB, DB — 20 minutes
Weights
Stretch

Saturday   Active Rest
Sunday   OFF DAY

WEEK TEN

Monday
  Stretch
  Fast Feet Timing Drills
  All Positions - 12 x 100 yards -
  Continuous movement, comfort-
  able stride pace. Every 200 yards,
  do 10 push ups

Tuesday
  Stretch
  Weights
  Stretch

Wednesday
  Stretch
  Fast Feet Timing Drills
  OL, DL - Jog 40 seconds, sprint 10
  seconds, repeat 10 times, continuous movement
  TE, LB, QB - Jog 40 seconds,
  sprint 10 seconds, repeat 12 times,
  continuous movement
  WR, RB, DB - Jog 40 seconds, sprint
  10 seconds, repeat 14 times,
  continuous movements

Thursday
  Stretch
  Weights
  Plyometrics
  Stretch

Friday
  Stretch
  Fast Feet Timing Drills
  Timed Run:
  OL, DL — 16 minutes
  TE, LB, QB — 18 minutes
  WR, RB, DB — 20 minutes
  Weights
  Stretch

Saturday   Active Rest
Sunday   OFF DAY

WEEK ELEVEN

Monday
  Stretch
  Fast Feet Timing Drills
  All Positions - 16 x 100 yards -
  Continuous movement, comfort-
  able stride pace. Every 200 yards,
  do 10 push ups

Tuesday
  Stretch
  Weights
  Stretch

Wednesday
  OFF FOR MINI CAMP

Thursday
  OFF

Friday
  OFF

Saturday   OFF
Sunday   OFF

PHASE II OF OFF-SEASON CONDITIONING:

BEGINNING OF INTERVAL TRAINING

WEEK TWELVE

Monday
Stretch
Fast Feet Timing Drills
Weights
Running Program:
  Jog 440
  Stretch
  Stride 330
  Walk 110
  Stride 220
  Walk 110
  Stride 220
  Walk 110
  Stride 110
  Walk 110
  Stride 110
  Walk 110
  Stride 110
  Walk 110
  Stride 110
  Walk 110
  Stretch

Tuesday
Stretch
Weights
Stretch

Wednesday
Stretch
Fast Feet Timing Drills
Running Program:
Stretch
10 x 110 yards sprint,
Walk 110 between each sprint
Target Times:
OL, DL — 16 seconds
TE, LB, QB — 15 seconds
WR, RB, DB — 14 seconds
Stretch

Thursday
Stretch
Plyometrics
Weights
Stretch

Friday
Stretch
Fast Feet Timing Drills
Weights
Running Program:
  Jog 440
  Stretch
  Stride 330
  Walk 110
  Stride 220
  Walk 110
  Stride 220
  Walk 110
  Stride 110
  Walk 110
  Stride 110
  Walk 110
  Stride 110
  Walk 110
  Stride 110
  Walk 110
  Stretch

Saturday   Active Rest
Sunday   OFF DAY

WEEK THIRTEEN

Monday

Stretch
Fast Feet Timing Drills
Weights
Running Program:
 Jog 440
 Stretch
 Stride 330
 Walk 110
 Stride 220
 Walk 110
 Stride 220
 Walk 110
 Stride 110
 Walk 110
 Stride 110
 Walk 110
 Stride 110
 Walk 110
 Stride 110
 Walk 110
 Stretch

Tuesday

Stretch
Weights
Stretch

Wednesday

Stretch
Fast Feet Timing Drills
Running Program:
 Stretch
 12 x 110 yards sprint
 Walk 110 between each
 sprint
Target Times:
OL, DL — 16 seconds
 TE, LB, QB — 15 seconds
WR, RB, DB — 14 seconds
Stretch

Thursday

Stretch
Plyometrics
Weights
Stretch

Friday

Stretch
Fast Feet Timing Drills
Weights
Running Program:
 Jog 440
 Stretch
 Stride 330
 Walk 110
 Stride 220
 Walk 110
 Stride 220
 Walk 110
 Stride 110
 Walk 110
 Stride 110
 Walk 110
 Stride 110
 Walk 110
 Stride 110
 Walk 110
 Stretch

Saturday   Active Rest
Sunday   OFF DAY

WEEK FOURTEEN

Monday
  Stretch
  Fast Feet Timing Drills
  Weights
  Running Program:
  Jog 440
  Stretch
  Stride 330
  Walk 110
  Stride 220
  Walk 110
  Stride 220
  Walk 110
  Stride 110
  Walk 110
  Stride 110
  Walk 110
  Stride 110
  Walk 110
  Stride 110
  Walk 110
  Stretch

Tuesday
  Stretch
  Weights
  Stretch

Wednesday
  Stretch
  Fast Feet Timing Drills
  Running Program:
  Stretch
  12 x 110 yards sprint
  Walk 110 between each sprint
  Target Times:
  OL, DL — 16 seconds
  TE, LB, QB — 15 seconds
  WR, RB, DB — 14 seconds
  Stretch

Thursday
  Stretch
  Plyometrics
  Weights
  Stretch

Friday
  Stretch
  Fast Feet Timing Drills
  Weights
  Running Program
  Jog 440
  Stretch
  Stride 330
  Walk 110
  Stride 220
  Walk 110
  Stride 220
  Walk 110
  Stride 110
  Walk 110
  Stride 110
  Walk 110
  Stride 110
  Walk 110
  Stride 110
  Walk 110
  Stretch

Saturday   Active Rest
Sunday   OFF DAY

WEEK FIFTEEN

Monday
Stretch
Fast Feet Timing Drills
Weights
Running Program:
  Jog 440
  Stretch
  Stride 220
  Jog 110
  Stride 220
  Jog 110
  Stride 110
  Jog 110
  Stride 110
  Walk 110
  Stride 110
  Walk 110
  Stride 110
  Walk 110
  Stride 110
  Walk 110
  Stretch

Tuesday
Stretch
Weights
Stretch

Wednesday
Stretch
Fast Feet Timing Drills
Running Program:
  Stretch
  12 x 110 yards sprint
  Walk 110 between each sprint
  Target Times:
  OL, DL – 15 seconds
  TE, LB, QB – 14 seconds
  WR, RB, DB 13 seconds

Thursday
Stretch
Plyometrics
Weights
Stretch

Friday
Stretch
Weights
Running Program:
  Jog 440
  Stretch
  Stride 330
  Walk 110
  Stride 220
  Jog 110
  Stride 220
  Walk 110
  Stride 110
  Walk 110
  Stride 110
  Walk 110
  Stride 110
  Walk 110
  Stride 110
  Walk 110
  Stride 110
  Walk 110
  Stretch

Saturday   Active Rest
Sunday   OFF DAY

AGILITY FORM PROGRAM

The following agility form program should be run after stretching and before each running workout.

You will need an area of grass or turf marked off 25 yards.

The workout is as follows:

- High Knee 2 x 25 yards, Rest 10 seconds
- Skip 2 x 25 yards, Rest 10 seconds
- Shuffle 2 x 25 yards, Rest 10 seconds
- Backward Sprint 2 x 25 yards, Rest 10 seconds
- Double Leg Hop (for speed) 2 x 25 yards, Rest 10 seconds
- Carioca 2 x 25 yards, Rest 2 minutes
- Begin Sprint routine

To obtain the full benefit of each of these drills, they must be run full speed with good form and total concentration.

SPRINT ROUTINE

For the remainder of your conditioning program, you will need to work on a marked, 100-yard football field. The emphasis during this phase of your training will be directed toward anaerobic sprint interval training. This portion of your training is very football-specific and will bring you into camp in excellent condition. This type of sprint training will facilitate speed improvement.

The 90-yard runs listed should be completed at the specific paces listed. Divide the field with markers into three 30-yard lengths.

Always complete the agility form drills prior to the sprint routine.

NOTE: FOR VAREITY, ONCE A WEEK YOU MAY SUBSTITUTE THE POSITION SPECIFIC PATTERN OUTLINED IN THE APPENDIX FOR THE SPRINT ROUTINE.

WEEK SIXTEEN

Monday

Jog 200 yards

Stretch

Agility form drills

Jog 30 yards, stride 30 yards, sprint 30 yards

Rest 15 seconds

Jog 30 yards, stride 30 yards, sprint 30 yards

Rest 15 seconds

Stride 30 yards, sprint 30 yards, stride 30 yards

Rest 15 seconds

Stride 30 yards, sprint 30 yards, stride 30 yards

Rest 15 seconds

Stride 30 yards, sprint 30 yards, stride 30 yards

Rest 15 seconds

Stride 30 yards, sprint 30 yards, stride 30 yards

Rest 15 seconds

Stride 90 yards

Rest 15 seconds

Sprint 90 yards

Rest 15 seconds

Stride 90 yards

Rest 15 seconds

Sprint 90 yards

Rest 15 seconds

Stride 30 yards, sprint 30 yards, stride 30 yards

Rest 15 seconds

Stride 30 yards, sprint 30 yards, stride 30 yards

Rest 15 seconds

Jog 30 yards, stride 30 yards, sprint 30 yards

Rest 15 seconds

Jog 30 yards, stride 30 yards, sprint 30 yards

Rest two minutes

Sprint 20 yards x 10 (no rest in-between)

Jog 200 yards

Stretch

Tuesday

Stretch

Weights

Stretch

Wednesday

Jog 200 yards

Stretch

Agility form drills

10 x 100 yards drills

Walk back 100 between each sprint

Rest two minutes

10 x 40 yard sprint

Walk back 40 between each sprint

Stretch

Thursday

Stretch

Fast Feet Timing Drills

Weights

Stretch

Friday

Jog 200 yards

Stretch

Agility form drills

Jog 30 yards, stride 30 yards, sprint 30 yards

Rest 15 seconds

Jog 30 yards, stride 30 yards, sprint 30 yards

Rest 15 seconds

Stride 30 yards, sprint 30 yards, stride 30 yards

Rest 15 seconds

Stride 30 yards, sprint 30 yards, stride 30 yards

Rest 15 seconds

Stride 30 yards, sprint 30 yards, stride 30 yards

Rest 15 seconds

Stride 30 yards, sprint 30 yards, stride 30 yards

Rest 15 seconds

Stride 90 yards

Rest 15 seconds

Sprint 90 yards
Rest 15 seconds
Stride 90 yards
Rest 15 seconds
Sprint 90 yards
Rest 15 seconds
Stride 30 yards, sprint 30 yards,
  stride 30 yards
Rest 15 seconds
Stride 30 yards, sprint 30 yards,
  stride 30 yards
Rest 15 seconds
Jog 30 yards, stride 30 yards, sprint
  30 yards
Rest 15 seconds
Jog 30 yards, stride 30 yards,
  sprint 30 yards
Rest two minutes
60 yard shuttle
Rest 30 seconds
60 yard shuttle
Rest 60 seconds
20 yard shuttle
Rest 30 seconds
20 yard shuttle
Jog 200 yards
Stretch

Saturday
Active Rest

Sunday
Stretch

WEEK SEVENTEEN

Monday
Jog 200 yards
Stretch
Agility form drills
Jog 30 yards, stride 30 yards, sprint
  30 yards
Rest 15 seconds
Jog 30 yards, stride 30 yards, sprint
  30 yards
Rest 15 seconds
Stride 30 yards, sprint 30 yards,
  stride 30 yards
Rest 15 seconds
Stride 30 yards, sprint 30 yards,
  stride 30 yards
Rest 15 seconds
Stride 30 yards, sprint 30 yards,
  stride 30 yards
Rest 15 seconds
Stride 30 yards, sprint 30 yards,
  stride 30 yards
Rest 15 seconds
Stride 90 yards
Rest 15 seconds
Sprint 90 yards
Rest 15 seconds
Stride 90 yards
Rest 15 seconds
Sprint 90 yards
Rest 15 seconds
Stride 30 yards, sprint 30 yards,
  stride 30 yards
Rest 15 seconds
Stride 30 yards, sprint 30 yards,
  stride 30 yards
Rest 15 seconds
Jog 30 yards, stride 30 yards, sprint
  30 yards
Rest 15 seconds
Jog 30 yards, stride 30 yards, sprint
  30 yards
Rest two minutes

Sprint 20 yards x 10 (no rest in-
between)
Jog 200 yards
Stretch

Tuesday
Stretch
Weights
Stretch

Wednesday
Jog 200 yards
Stretch
Agility form drills
12 x 100 yards drills
Walk back 100 between each sprint
Rest two minutes
10 x 40 yard sprint
Walk back 40 between each sprint
Stretch

Thursday
Stretch
Fast Feet Timing Drills
Weights
Stretch

Friday
Jog 200 yards
Stretch
Agility form drills
Jog 30 yards, stride 30 yards, sprint
30 yards
Rest 15 seconds
Jog 30 yards, stride 30 yards, sprint
30 yards
Rest 15 seconds
Stride 30 yards, sprint 30 yards,
stride 30 yards
Rest 15 seconds
Stride 30 yards, sprint 30 yards,
stride 30 yards
Rest 15 seconds
Stride 30 yards, sprint 30 yards,
stride 30 yards
Rest 15 seconds

Stride 30 yards, sprint 30 yards,
stride 30 yards
Rest 15 seconds
Stride 90 yards
Rest 15 seconds
Sprint 90 yards
Rest 15 seconds
Stride 90 yards
Rest 15 seconds
Sprint 90 yards
Rest 15 seconds
Stride 30 yards, sprint 30 yards,
stride 30 yards
Rest 15 seconds
Stride 30 yards, sprint 30 yards,
stride 30 yards
Rest 15 seconds
Jog 30 yards, stride 30 yards, sprint
30 yards
Rest 15 seconds
Jog 30 yards, stride 30 yards, sprint
30 yards
Rest two minutes
Sprint 30 yards x 10 (10 second rest
in-between)
Jog 200 yards
Stretch

Saturday
Active Rest

Sunday
Stretch

WEEK EIGHTEEN

Monday

Jog 200 yards

Stretch

Agility form drills

Jog 30 yards, stride 30 yards, sprint 30 yards

Rest 15 seconds

Jog 30 yards, stride 30 yards, sprint 30 yards

Rest 15 seconds

Stride 30 yards, sprint 30 yards, stride 30 yards

Rest 15 seconds

Stride 30 yards, sprint 30 yards, stride 30 yards

Rest 15 seconds

Stride 30 yards, sprint 30 yards, stride 30 yards

Rest 15 seconds

Stride 30 yards, sprint 30 yards, stride 30 yards

Rest 15 seconds

Stride 90 yards

Rest 15 seconds

Sprint 90 yards

Rest 15 seconds

Stride 90 yards

Rest 15 seconds

Sprint 90 yards

Rest 15 seconds

Stride 30 yards, sprint 30 yards, stride 30 yards

Rest 15 seconds

Stride 30 yards, sprint 30 yards, stride 30 yards

Rest 15 seconds

Jog 30 yards, stride 30 yards, sprint 30 yards

Rest 15 seconds

Jog 30 yards, stride 30 yards, sprint 30 yards

Rest two minutes

Sprint 30 yards x 10 (10 second rest in-between)

Jog 200 yards

Stretch

Weights

Stretch

Tuesday

Stretch

Weights

Stretch

Wednesday

Jog 200 yards

Stretch

Agility form drills

12 x 100 yards drills

Walk back 100 between each sprint

Rest two minutes

10 x 40 yard sprint

Walk back 40 between each sprint

Stretch

Thursday

Stretch

Fast Feet Timing Drills

Weights

Stretch

Friday

Jog 200 yards

Stretch

Agility form drills

Jog 30 yards, stride 30 yards, sprint 30 yards

Rest 15 seconds

Jog 30 yards, stride 30 yards, sprint 30 yards

Rest 15 seconds

Stride 30 yards, sprint 30 yards, stride 30 yards

Rest 15 seconds

Stride 30 yards, sprint 30 yards, stride 30 yards

Rest 15 seconds

Stride 30 yards, sprint 30 yards, stride 30 yards

Rest 15 seconds

Stride 30 yards, sprint 30 yards,
  stride 30 yards
Rest 15 seconds
Stride 90 yards
Rest 15 seconds
Sprint 90 yards
Rest 15 seconds
Stride 90 yards
Rest 15 seconds
Sprint 90 yards
Rest 15 seconds
Stride 30 yards, sprint 30 yards,
  stride 30 yards
Rest 15 seconds
Stride 30 yards, sprint 30 yards,
  stride 30 yards
Rest 15 seconds
Jog 30 yards, stride 30 yards, sprint
  30 yards
Rest 15 seconds
Jog 30 yards, stride 30 yards, sprint
  30 yards
Rest two minutes
Sprint 30 yards x 10 (10 second rest
  in-between)
Jog 200 yards
Stretch

Saturday
Active Rest

Sunday
Stretch

WEEK NINETEEN

Monday
Jog 200 yards
Stretch
Agility form drills
Jog 30 yards, stride 30 yards, sprint
  30 yards
Rest 15 seconds
Jog 30 yards, stride 30 yards, sprint
  30 yards
Rest 15 seconds
Stride 30 yards, sprint 30 yards,
  stride 30 yards
Rest 15 seconds
Stride 30 yards, sprint 30 yards,
  stride 30 yards
Rest 15 seconds
Stride 30 yards, sprint 30 yards,
  stride 30 yards
Rest 15 seconds
Stride 30 yards, sprint 30 yards,
  stride 30 yards
Rest 15 seconds
Stride 90 yards
Rest 15 seconds
Sprint 90 yards
Rest 15 seconds
Stride 90 yards
Rest 15 seconds
Sprint 90 yards
Rest 15 seconds
Stride 30 yards, sprint 30 yards,
  stride 30 yards
Rest 15 seconds
Stride 30 yards, sprint 30 yards,
  stride 30 yards
Rest 15 seconds
Jog 30 yards, stride 30 yards, sprint
  30 yards
Rest 15 seconds
Jog 30 yards, stride 30 yards, sprint
  30 yards
Rest two minutes
Sprint 30 yards x 10
  (10 second rest in-between)
Jog 200 yards

Stretch
Weights
Stretch

Tuesday
Stretch
Weights
Stretch

Wednesday
Jog 200 yards
Stretch
Agility form drills
12 x 100 yards drills
Walk back 100 between each sprint
Rest two minutes
10 x 40 yard sprint
Walk back 40 between each sprint
Stretch

Thursday
Stretch
Fast Feet Timing Drills
Weights
Stretch

Friday
Jog 200 yards
Stretch
Agility form drills
Jog 30 yards, stride 30 yards, sprint 30 yards
Rest 15 seconds
Jog 30 yards, stride 30 yards, sprint 30 yards
Rest 15 seconds
Stride 30 yards, sprint 30 yards, stride 30 yards
Rest 15 seconds
Stride 30 yards, sprint 30 yards, stride 30 yards
Rest 15 seconds
Stride 30 yards, sprint 30 yards, stride 30 yards
Rest 15 seconds

Stride 30 yards, sprint 30 yards, stride 30 yards
Rest 15 seconds
Stride 90 yards
Rest 15 seconds
Sprint 90 yards
Rest 15 seconds
Stride 90 yards
Rest 15 seconds
Sprint 90 yards
Rest 15 seconds
Stride 30 yards, sprint 30 yards, stride 30 yards
Rest 15 seconds
Stride 30 yards, sprint 30 yards, stride 30 yards
Rest 15 seconds
Jog 30 yards, stride 30 yards, sprint 30 yards
Rest 15 seconds
Jog 30 yards, stride 30 yards, sprint 30 yards
Rest two minutes
Sprint 30 yards x 10 (10 second rest in-between)
Jog 200 yards
Stretch

Saturday
Active Rest

Sunday
Stretch

WEEK TWENTY

Monday

Jog 200 yards

Stretch

Agility form drills

Jog 30 yards, stride 30 yards, sprint 30 yards

Rest 15 seconds

Jog 30 yards, stride 30 yards, sprint 30 yards

Rest 15 seconds

Stride 30 yards, sprint 30 yards, stride 30 yards

Rest 15 seconds

Stride 30 yards, sprint 30 yards, stride 30 yards

Rest 15 seconds

Stride 30 yards, sprint 30 yards, stride 30 yards

Rest 15 seconds

Stride 30 yards, sprint 30 yards, stride 30 yards

Rest 15 seconds

Stride 90 yards

Rest 15 seconds

Sprint 90 yards

Rest 15 seconds

Stride 90 yards

Rest 15 seconds

Sprint 90 yards

Rest 15 seconds

Stride 30 yards, sprint 30 yards, stride 30 yards

Rest 15 seconds

Stride 30 yards, sprint 30 yards, stride 30 yards

Rest 15 seconds

Jog 30 yards, stride 30 yards, sprint 30 yards

Rest 15 seconds

Jog 30 yards, stride 30 yards, sprint 30 yards

Rest two minutes

Sprint 40 yards x 8 (10-second rest in-between)

Rest one minute

20 yard shuttle x 3 (30 second rest in-between)

Jog 200 yards

Stretch

Weights

Stretch

Tuesday

Stretch

Weights

Stretch

Wednesday

Jog 200 yards

Stretch

Agility form drills

12 x 100 yards drills

Walk back 100 between each sprint

Rest two minutes

10 x 40 yard sprint

Walk back 40 between each sprint

Stretch

Thursday

Stretch

Fast Feet Timing Drills

Weights

Stretch

Friday

Jog 200 yards

Stretch

Agility form drills

Jog 30 yards, stride 30 yards, sprint 30 yards

Rest 15 seconds

Jog 30 yards, stride 30 yards, sprint 30 yards

Rest 15 seconds

Stride 30 yards, sprint 30 yards, stride 30 yards

Rest 15 seconds

Stride 30 yards, sprint 30 yards, stride 30 yards

Rest 15 seconds

Stride 30 yards, sprint 30 yards, stride 30 yards

Rest 15 seconds

Stride 30 yards, sprint 30 yards, stride 30 yards

Rest 15 seconds

Stride 90 yards

Rest 15 seconds

Sprint 90 yards

Rest 15 seconds

Stride 90 yards

Rest 15 seconds

Sprint 90 yards

Rest 15 seconds

Stride 30 yards, sprint 30 yards, stride 30 yards

Rest 15 seconds

Stride 30 yards, sprint 30 yards, stride 30 yards

Rest 15 seconds

Jog 30 yards, stride 30 yards, sprint 30 yards

Rest 15 seconds

Jog 30 yards, stride 30 yards, sprint 30 yards

Rest two minutes

Sprint 40 yards x 8 (10 second rest in-between)

Rest one minute

20-yard shuttle x 3 (30 second rest in-between)

Jog 200 yards

Stretch

Saturday

Stretch

Sunday

Active Rest

WEEK TWENTY-ONE

Monday

Jog 200 yards

Stretch

Agility form drills

Jog 30 yards, stride 30 yards, sprint 30 yards

Rest 15 seconds

Jog 30 yards, stride 30 yards, sprint 30 yards

Rest 15 seconds

Stride 30 yards, sprint 30 yards, stride 30 yards

Rest 15 seconds

Stride 30 yards, sprint 30 yards, stride 30 yards

Rest 15 seconds

Stride 30 yards, sprint 30 yards, stride 30 yards

Rest 15 seconds

Stride 30 yards, sprint 30 yards, stride 30 yards

Rest 15 seconds

Stride 90 yards

Rest 15 seconds

Sprint 90 yards

Rest 15 seconds

Stride 90 yards

Rest 15 seconds

Sprint 90 yards

Rest 15 seconds

Stride 30 yards, sprint 30 yards, stride 30 yards

Rest 15 seconds

Stride 30 yards, sprint 30 yards, stride 30 yards

Rest 15 seconds

Jog 30 yards, stride 30 yards, sprint 30 yards

Rest 15 seconds

Jog 30 yards, stride 30 yards, sprint 30 yards

Rest two minutes

Sprint 40 yards x 8 (10 second rest in-between)

Rest one minute
20 yard shuttle x 3 (30 second rest in-between)
Jog 200 yards
Stretch
Weights
Stretch

Tuesday
Stretch
Weights
Stretch

Wednesday
Jog 200 yards
Stretch
Agility form drills
12 x 100 yards drills
Walk back 100 between each sprint
Rest two minutes
10 x 40 yard sprint
Walk back 40 between each sprint
Stretch

Thursday
Stretch
Fast Feet Timing Drills
Weights
Stretch

Friday
Jog 200 yards
Stretch
Agility form drills
Jog 30 yards, stride 30 yards, sprint 30 yards
Rest 15 seconds
Jog 30 yards, stride 30 yards, sprint 30 yards
Rest 15 seconds
Stride 30 yards, sprint 30 yards, stride 30 yards
Rest 15 seconds
Stride 30 yards, sprint 30 yards, stride 30 yards
Rest 15 seconds

Stride 30 yards, sprint 30 yards, stride 30 yards
Rest 15 seconds
Stride 30 yards, sprint 30 yards, stride 30 yards
Rest 15 seconds
Stride 90 yards
Rest 15 seconds
Sprint 90 yards
Rest 15 seconds
Stride 90 yards
Rest 15 seconds
Sprint 90 yards
Rest 15 seconds
Stride 30 yards, sprint 30 yards, stride 30 yards
Rest 15 seconds
Stride 30 yards, sprint 30 yards, stride 30 yards
Rest 15 seconds
Jog 30 yards, stride 30 yards, sprint 30 yards
Rest 15 seconds
Jog 30 yards, stride 30 yards, sprint 30 yards
Rest two minutes
Sprint 40 yards x 8 (10 second rest in-between)
Rest one minute
20-yard shuttle x 3 (30 second rest in-between)
Jog 200 yards
Stretch

Saturday
Stretch

Sunday
Active Rest

WEEK TWENTY-TWO

Monday (LAST RUN)

Jog 200 yards

Stretch

Agility form drills

Jog 30 yards, stride 30 yards, sprint
30 yards

Rest 15 seconds

Jog 30 yards, stride 30 yards, sprint
30 yards

Rest 15 seconds

Stride 30 yards, sprint 30 yards,
stride 30 yards

Rest 15 seconds

Stride 30 yards, sprint 30 yards,
stride 30 yards

Rest 15 seconds

Stride 30 yards, sprint 30 yards,
stride 30 yards

Rest 15 seconds

Stride 30 yards, sprint 30 yards,
stride 30 yards

Rest 15 seconds

Stride 90 yards

Rest 15 seconds

Sprint 90 yards

Rest 15 seconds

Stride 90 yards

Rest 15 seconds

Sprint 90 yards

Rest 15 seconds

Stride 30 yards, sprint 30 yards,
stride 30 yards

Rest 15 seconds

Stride 30 yards, sprint 30 yards,
stride 30 yards

Rest 15 seconds   .

Jog 30 yards, stride 30 yards, sprint
30 yards

Rest 15 seconds

Jog 30 yards, stride 30 yards, sprint
30 yards

Rest two minutes

Sprint 40 yards x 8 (10 second rest
in-between)

Rest one minute

20-yard shuttle x 3 (30 second rest
in-between)

Jog 200 yards

Stretch

Tuesday

Training camp begins

Stretch

Weights

Stretch

Wednesday

Jog 200 yards

Stretch

Agility form drills

12 x 100 yard sprint

Walk back 100 between each sprint

Rest two minutes

10 x 40 yard sprint

Walk back 40 between each sprint

10 x 10 yard sprint

Walk back 10 between each sprint

Stretch

Thursday

Stretch

Fast Feet Timing Drills

Weights

Stretch

Friday

Jog 200 yards

Stretch

Agility form drills

Jog 30 yards, stride 30 yards, sprint
30 yards

Rest 15 seconds

Jog 30 yards, stride 30 yards, sprint
30 yards

Rest 15 seconds

Stride 30 yards, sprint 30 yards,
stride 30 yards

Rest 15 seconds

Stride 30 yards, sprint 30 yards,
stride 30 yards

Rest 15 seconds

120

Stride 30 yards, sprint 30 yards, stride 30 yards

Rest 15 seconds

Stride 30 yards, sprint 30 yards, stride 30 yards

Rest 15 seconds

Stride 90 yards

Rest 15 seconds

Sprint 90 yards

Rest 15 seconds

Stride 90 yards

Rest 15 seconds

Sprint 90 yards

Rest 15 seconds

Stride 30 yards, sprint 30 yards, stride 30 yards

Rest 15 seconds

Stride 30 yards, sprint 30 yards, stride 30 yards

Rest 15 seconds

Jog 30 yards, stride 30 yards, sprint 30 yards

Rest 15 seconds

Jog 30 yards, stride 30 yards, sprint 30 yards

Rest two minutes

Sprint 40 yards x 8 (10 second rest in-between)

Rest one minute

20-yard shuttle x 3 (30 second rest in-between)

Jog 200 yards

Stretch

Weights

Stretch

Saturday

Stretch

Sunday

OFF DAY

10 NUTRITION

The body burns three fuels for energy — protein, carbohydrates, and fats.

PROTEIN

Protein affects the growth and maintenance of all body tissue. It is a major source of building material for muscle, all of the internal organs, blood, skin, hair, and nails. Protein also plays a vital role in the formation of hormones, including testosterone. Once digested, protein is broken down into amino acids. Amino acids are the end products of protein digestion. After they're broken down, amino acids enter an amino acid pool and they are stored along with other amino acids from previous meals. The body then draws upon the pool constantly when new protein is needed for tissue repair or for cell growth.

The body requires approximately 21 amino acids to manufacture new protein. Eleven of these amino acids are manufactured in the body from any source of nitrogen. Ten that cannot be produced in the body are called the essential amino acids. They come from our diet. For the body to properly utilize protein, all of the essential amino acids have to be present at the same time in the proper proportions. If any one of these amino acids is missing, protein synthesis will move to a very slow level or cease totally. The result is that all amino acids present are reduced in proportion to the amino acid that is the low or missing amino acid.

Nonessential Amino Acids (Amino acids manufactured within the body.)

1. Alanine	7. Hydroxyproline
2. Aspartic Acid	8. Hydroxylamine
3. Cysteine	9. Proline
4. Cystine	10. Serine
5. Glutamic Acid	11. Tyrosine
6. Glycine	

Essential Amino Acids (Amino acids we must have in the diet.)

1. Arginine	6. Phenylalanine
2. Isoleucine	7. Phreonine
3. Leucine	8. Tryptophan
4. Lysine	9. Valine
5. Methionine	10. Histidine

The Protein Dilemma: How Much is Enough?

Too little protein in the diet causes slow recovery from hard training, a low energy level, poor resistance to infection and poor muscle tone. How much protein does an athlete need on a regular training regimen? If we all ate a well-balanced diet, four meals a day, with the proper combination of carbohydrates, protein and fats, no additional protein supplementation would be necessary.

Unfortunately, very few of us do this.

If an athlete is on a rigorous training schedule and fails to take in the required amount of protein to rebuild his muscle tissue, he quickly will fall into the category of overtraining. His recovery will be impaired and he might actually harm himself with his training.

A general rule of thumb is that an athlete should take in one gram of protein per day per two pounds of body weight. For example, a 300-pound athlete needs to spread 150 grams of good protein over his day's dietary intake. Remember, all of the amino acids are needed to provide the body with top quality protein. Foods that are complete proteins are meat, fish, chicken, dairy products, eggs and soybeans. The bulk of your protein intake should come from the foods you eat, but if supplementation is necessary to receive the required amount of protein, then so be it.

Remember, the body works on a priority system. If the internal organs require protein for rebuilding and repair, the muscle will be starved of protein that is present in the body. It is imperative that the athlete on a hard training regimen follow this one gram per two pounds of body weight strictly.

CARBOHYDRATES

Carbohydrates are the most readily available source of fuel for the athlete. After carbohydrates have completed the digestion process, they are transported by the blood stream to the liver, where they are converted to glucose. The glucose is then carried by the blood stream to provide energy for muscle and the brain. A small amount of this glucose is converted to glycogen and stored in the muscles and liver.

Glycogen is the most important fuel for athletes because it is the most readily available energy source. An athlete deficient in carbohydrates will experience rapid depletion of those glycogen stores, which makes physical activity very difficult. That fatigued feeling after prolonged exercise is often due to low blood sugar and depleted glycogen stores. A low carbohydrate diet or a fast makes extensive exercise extremely difficult, if not impossible.

An athlete working on an intensive training program should increase his complex carbohydrate intake. Foods that contain these properties are grains, breads, pasta, potatoes, vegetables, and fruits. Again, if your diet lacks in these components, supplementation may be necessary through high carbohydrate drinks of which a variety are on the market today.

FATS

A popular misconception among athletes is that fat should be totally removed from the diet. Dietary fat is the most concentrated source of energy in the diet. When oxidized, dietary fat provides more than twice the calories per gram as those furnished by protein or carbohydrates.

Fats are necessary in our diet. Besides a concentrated source of energy, they act as carriers for fat soluble vitamins, they surround and protect vital organs, and they preserve body heat. However, an overabundance of fat intake is not desirable for an athlete. Studies have shown that excess body fat slows the athlete's muscle-firing capabilities, and generally causes the athlete to fatigue quicker than the leaner athlete.

Moderation is the key. Fat intake should comprise no more than 15 percent of your daily calories.

VITAMINS AND MINERALS

Vitamins and minerals are essential for life. Unlike amino acids, they cannot be made by the body. Vitamins are present in varying quantities in the foods that we eat. They're essential for growth, health and recovery.

Vitamins and minerals set the stage for protein synthesis, carbohydrate and fat digestion and energy production. Vitamins enable all the necessary reactions to take place to convert the food into energy and assist in the forming of bone and tissue. Every vitamin and mineral has a specific task that no other substance can accomplish. The absence of all or part of any vitamin or mineral can disrupt the biomechanical reactions necessary to enable the body to fully recover and carry on its normal function.

Again, if a diet is perfectly balanced, no supplementation of vitamins or minerals is necessary, but remember that balance comes through very few of the things that we eat. A vitamin-mineral pack on a daily basis is a good idea for an athlete training to be his best.

WATER

The days of suffering through two-a-day practices while the coach withholds water as a "toughness exercise" are gone. Water is the most essential ingredient that an athlete can consume. You can go much longer without food than without water. The average adult body contains about 11 gallons of water. About 50 percent of our body weight is water. Depleting these water stores through activ-

There is only one way to avoid criticism: say nothing, do nothing, be nothing

ity, especially strenuous activity, doesn't enable the body to perform at its highest capabilities. Water should be consumed throughout the day — prior to a heavy workout, during the workout and immediately after the workout. It's impossible for an athlete to drink too much water.

SUMMARY

As an athlete or coach, you must look at the human body as a finely-tuned race car. Without fuel, the car simply coasts to a stop short of its goal. Every athlete must make a conscious effort to stock his body with the proper fuel. Intelligent choices in your eating, discipline, proper rest, and recovery are all ingredients for success.

Diet is a totally controllable process. Any athlete who falls short of protein, carbohydrate or fat requirements shows a lack of knowledge or a lack of discipline. Supplementation is a widely accepted form of dietary enhancement. Remember, what you put in your body dictates your potential for growth, recovery, and success.

NUTRITIONAL GUIDELINES

1. Protein should comprise 35 percent of your daily calories. Don't overdo or underdo the consumption of protein in your diet. It is the building block of your system. One gram of protein for every two pounds of body weight will be sufficient.

2. Carbohydrates should comprise 50 percent of your daily calories. Remember, carbohydrates are the most readily available source of energy for the human body. Whole grains, fruits and vegetables are the food that contain these complex carbohydrates. Stay away from simple sugars; they cause drastic high/low swings in your insulin levels.

3. Fats should comprise 15 percent of your daily calories. Limit your intake of the saturated fats, heavily marbled meats, whole milk. Choose the leaner cuts of beef, pull the skin off the chicken, and bake (rather than fry) the fish. Fat is essential, but your body fat percentage should always be kept in check. Last, but not least, be a student of your diet and know what you put in your body and why.

Remember, your body is your key to success.

APPENDIX: PATTERN RUN PROGRESSIONS

Explanation of Exercises:

Each progression is to be done in pairs, with the players taking turns reading the instructions and executing the patterns (one reads the instructions aloud, the other performs the drill and then they switch places). After both players have success-fully executed one pattern in the progression, they will move on to the next pattern.

Select a starting spot on the field. All patterns in a set will begin from that spot. Between each full speed pattern, jog back to that spot to begin the next pattern. Your running partner will call out your next pattern to you during your jog back to that spot until you finish 10 consecutive patterns. Begin each pattern from your position stance. On all pass routes, make sure all breaks are the proper depth from the line of scrimmage.

Note: The clock should run continuously from the time you initiate the first step in the pattern until you jog back and touch the spot after the last step. Target time should be two minutes and 45 seconds or less. Rest interval between each pattern is two minutes and 45 seconds (or as long as it takes your partner to finish the pattern).

DEFENSIVE LINE PATTERN RUN PROGRESSION

Set 1 Patterns
1. 10 yards shuffle right
2. 5 yards straight ahead
3. 40 yards straight ahead
4. 15 yards straight ahead
5. 10 yards shuffle left
6. Sprint 3 yards upfield, turn right and sprint 20 yards
7. 40 yards straight ahead
8. 5 yards straight ahead
9. Sprint 3 yards upfield, turn left and sprint 20 yards
10. 15 yards straight ahead

Set 2 Patterns
1. 40 yards straight ahead
2. 15 yards straight ahead
3. 10 yards shuffle left
4. 10 yards shuffle right
5. 5 yards straight ahead
6. 40 yards straight ahead
7. Sprint 3 yards upfield , turn right and sprint 20 yards
8. 15 yards straight ahead
9. Sprint 3 yards upfield, turn left and sprint 20 yards
10. 40 yards straight ahead

Set 3 Patterns
1. 15 yards straight ahead
2. 5 yards straight ahead
3. Sprint 3 yards upfield, turn right and sprint 20 yards
4. 40 yards straight ahead
5. 15 yards straight ahead
6. Sprint 3 yards upfield, turn left and sprint 20 yards
7. 40 yards straight ahead
8. 5 yards straight ahead
9. 10 yards shuffle right
10. 15 yards straight ahead

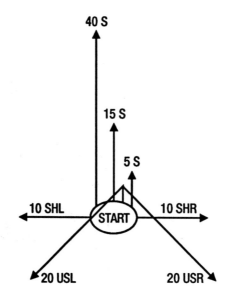

LINEBACKER PATTERN RUN PROGRESSION

Set 1 Patterns

1. 5 yards straight ahead
2. 3 shuffles right and sprint 10 yards
3. 12 yards drop left
4. 40 yards drop left
5. 5 yards backpedal, 5 yards forward
6. 3 shuffles left and sprint 10 yards
7. 15 yards backpedal
8. 12 yards drop right
9. 5 yards backpedal, crossover run 2 times right and left for 5 yards each time, then turn and sprint for 5 yards
10. 20 yards straight ahead

Set 2 Patterns

1. 5 yards backpedal, 5 yards forward
2. 12 yards drop left
3. 3 shuffles left and sprint 10 yards
4. 5 yards backpedal, crossover run 2 times right and left for 5 yards each time, then turn and sprint for 5 yards
5. 5 yards straight ahead
6. 20 yards straight ahead
7. 15 yards backpedal
8. 3 shuffles left and sprint 10 yards
9. 40 yards straight ahead
10. 15 yards backpedal

Set 3 Patterns

1. 3 shuffles left and sprint 10 yards
2. 3 shuffles right and sprint 10 yards
3. 5 yards backpedal, 5 yards forward
4. 40 yards straight ahead
5. 40 yards straight ahead
6. 23 yards drop right
7. 4 yards straight ahead
8. 5 yards backpedal, crossover run 2 times right and left for 5 yards each, then turn and sprint for 5 yards
9. 20 yards straight ahead
10. 15 yards backpedal

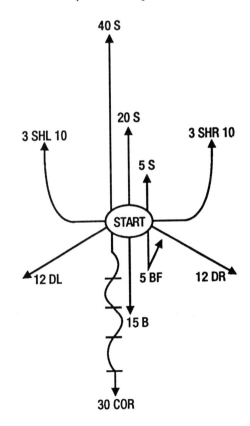

OFFENSIVE LINE PATTERN RUN PROGRESSION

Set 1 Patterns

1. Drop step, sprint 5 yards straight ahead
2. Drop step, sprint 40 yards straight ahead
3. 15 yards pull right
4. Drop step, sprint 10 yards straight
5. 20 yards back shuffle
6. 10 yards shuffle left
7. 15 yards pull left
8. 10 yards shuffle right
9. Drop step, sprint 40 yards straight ahead
10. 5 yards pass set

Set 2 Patterns

1. Drop step, sprint 40 yards straight ahead
2. Drop step, sprint 10 yards straight ahead
3. 10 yards shuffle right
4. 20 yards back shuffle
5. 5 yards pass set
6. 15 yards pull left
7. Drop step, sprint 40 yards straight ahead
8. 5 yards pass set
9. 15 yards pull right
10. 10 yards shuffle left

Set 3 Patterns

1. Drop step, sprint 10 yards straight ahead
2. 15 yards pull left
3. Drop step, sprint 40 yards straight ahead
4. Drop step, sprint 40 yards straight ahead
5. 10 yards shuffle left
6. 20 yards back shuffle
7. 5 yards pass set
8. 15 yards pull right
9. 10 yards shuffle left
10. 15 yards pull left

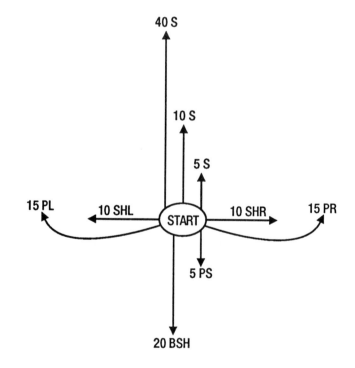

DEFENSIVE BACKS PATTERN RUN PROGRESSION

Set 1 Patterns

1. 20 yards backpedal
2. Zone drill: crossover run at 45 degree angle left for 10 yards. Square up and backpedal for 5 yards. Break at a 90 degree angle for 5 yards left
3. 40 yards straight ahead
4. 10 yards backpedal, break left
5. 5 yards backpedal, 10 yards straight ahead
6. Cushion drill: backpedal 10 yards, turn left and sprint 5 yards, then break left or straight back
7. 10 yards backpedal, break right
8. Flag drill: backpedal 10 yards, crossover run left at a 45 degree angle for 5 yards, wheel out and sprint 5 yards
9. Cushion drill: backpedal 10 yards, turn right and sprint 5 yards then break right or straight back
10. 10 yards straight ahead

Set 2 Patterns

1. 40 yards straight ahead
2. 10 yards backpedal, break right
3. 5 yards backpedal, 10 yards straight ahead
4. Zone drill: crossover run at 45 degree angle left for 10 yards. Square up and backpedal for 5 yards. Break at a 90 degree angle for 5 yards left
5. 20 yards backpedal
6. Flag drill: backpedal 10 yards, crossover run left at a 45 degree angle for 5 yards, wheel out and sprint 5 yards
7. Cushion drill: backpedal 10 yards, turn right and sprint 5 yards then break right or straight back
8. 10 yards backpedal, break left
9. Zone drill: crossover run at 45 degree angle left for 10 yards. Square up and backpedal for 5 yards. Break at a 90 degree angle for 5 yards left
10. 20 yards straight ahead

Set 3 Patterns

1. 10 yards backpedal, break left
2. Flag drill: backpedal 10 yards, crossover run left at a 45 degree angle for 5 yards, wheel out and sprint 5 yards
3. 20 yards straight ahead
4. Cushion drill: backpedal 10 yards, turn right and sprint 5 yards then break right or straight back
5. 20 yards backpedal
6. 10 yards backpedal, break right
7. 5 yards backpedal, 10 yards straight ahead
8. Zone drill: crossover run at 45 degree angle left for 10 yards. Square up and backpedal for 5 yards. Break at a 90 degree angle for 5 yards left
9. Flag drill: backpedal 10 yards, crossover run left at a 45 degree angle for 5 yards, wheel out and sprint 5 yards
10. 10 yards straight ahead

Diagram on following page

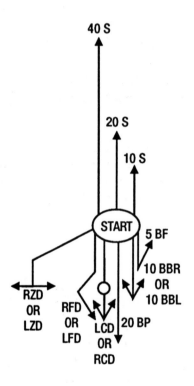

TIGHT END PATTERN RUN PROGRESSION

Set 1 Patterns
1. Over right (man)
2. Middle read right (man)
3. Option right (man)
4. Post right (40 yards)
5. Sneak right
6. Over left (man)
7. Middle read left (man)
8. Option left (man)
9. Post left (40 yards)
10. Sneak left

Set 2 Patterns
1. Bench right
2. Snap right
3. In right
4. Post right (40 yards)
5. Option right (zone)
6. Bench left
7. Snag left
8. In left
9. Post left (10 yards)
10. Option left (zone)

Set 3 Patterns
1. Middle area right (zone)
2. Over right (zone)
3. Bench right
4. Snag right
5. Sneak right
6. Middle read left (zone)
7. Over left (zone)
8. Bench left
9. Snag left
10. Sneak left

Additional Instructions: On all pass routes make sure all breaks are the proper depth from the line of scrimmage. Realize that you will be running these routes to the right and to the left side of the formation. When you change from routes on the right side to the left side, just turn and face the opposite direction in the same spot on the field. Also on pass routes the caller will state the defender is man or zone, and then you must make any route adjustments.

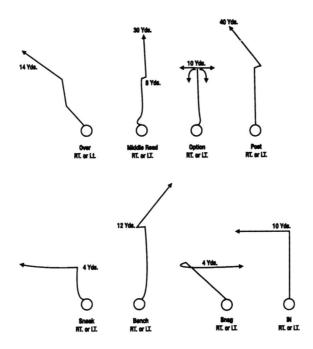

WIDE RECEIVER PATTERN RUN PROGRESSION

Set 1 Patterns

1. Drop step, sprint 5 yards straight ahead
2. Drop step, sprint 40 yards straight ahead
3. 15 yards pull right
4. Drop step, sprint 10 yards straight
5. 20 yards back shuffle
6. 10 yards shuffle left
7. 15 yards pull left
8. 10 yards shuffle right
9. Drop step, sprint 40 yards straight ahead
10. 5 yards pass set

Set 2 Patterns

1. Drop step, sprint 40 yards straight ahead
2. Drop step, sprint 10 yards straight ahead
3. 10 yards shuffle right
4. 20 yards back shuffle
5. 5 yards pass set
6. 15 yards pull left
7. Drop step, sprint 40 yards straight ahead
8. 5 yards pass set
9. 15 yards pull right
10. 10 yards shuffle left

Set 3 Patterns

1. Drop step, sprint 10 yards straight ahead
2. 15 yards pull left
3. Drop step, sprint 40 yards straight ahead
4. Drop step, sprint 40 yards straight ahead
5. 10 yards shuffle left
6. 20 yards back shuffle
7. 5 yards pass set
8. 15 yards pull right
9. 10 yards shuffle left
10. 15 yards pull left

Additional Instructions: On all pass routes make sure all breaks are the proper depth from the line of scrimmage. Realize that you will be running these routes to the right and to the left side of the formation. When you change from routes on the right side to the left side, just turn and face the opposite direction in the same spot on the field. On all patterns mentally place a defender in an inside or an outside technique and in a press or off position. Make your route adjustments according to the defender's alignment. Take the proper splits on each route. Imagine the ball in the middle of the field.

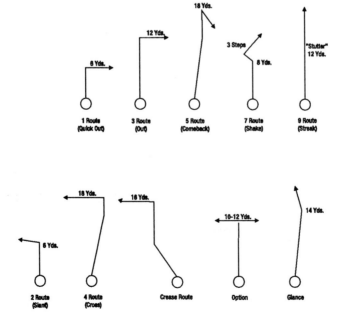

FULLBACK PATTERN RUN PROGRESSION

Set 1 Patterns

1. Fan right (man)
2. Wide right (20 yards)
3. Run zig zag (30 yards)
4. Option right (outside technique, man)
5. Fan left (man)
6. Wide left (20 yards)
7. Close right (20 yards)
8. Bench right (10 yards)
9. Screen right (20 yards)
10. Option left (outside technique, man)

Set 2 Patterns

1. Close left (20 yards)
2. Option left (zone)
3. Screen left (20 yards)
4. Run zig zag (30 yards)
5. Close right (20 yards)
6. Bench left (10 yards)
7. Screen right (20 yards)
8. Wide right (20 yards)
9. Fan left (zone)
10. Bench right (10 yards)

Set 3 Patterns

1. Fan zig zag (30 yards)
2. Fan right (zone)
3. Wide left (20 yards)
4. Option right (zone)
5. Run zig zag (30 yards)
6. Close left (20 yards)
7. Bench left (10 yards)
8. Screen left (20 yards)
9. Backs cross right (20 yards)
10. Backs cross left (20 yards)

Additional Instructions: On all pass routes make sure all breaks are the proper depth from the line of scrimmage. Realize that you will be running these routes to the right and to the left side of the formation. Also, on pass routes the caller will state the defender is man, inside, outside technique or zone and then you must make your route adjustments.

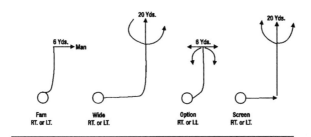

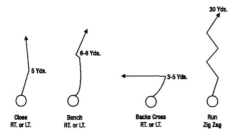

HALFBACK PATTERN RUN PROGRESSION

Set 1 Patterns

1. HB - fan right (man)
2. HB - wide right (20 yards)
3. HB - swing right
4. HB - option right (outside
   · technique, man)
5. HB - screen right (20 yards)
6. HB - fan left (man)
7. HB - wide left (20 yards)
8. HB - swing left
9. HB - option right (outside technique, man)
10. HB - screen left (20 yards)

Set 2 Patterns

1. IR - bench right
2. IR - option right (zone)
3. HB - zig zag run (30 yards)
4. WR - hinge right
5. WR - out right
6. IR - Bench left
7. IR - Option left (zone)
8. HB - zig zag run (30 yards)
9. WR - hinge left
10. WR - out left

Set 3 Patterns

1. WR - hinge right
2. WR - out right
3. WR - comeback right
4. WR - streak right (40 yards)
5. HB - zig zag run (30 yards)
6. WR - hinge left
7. WR - out left
8. WR - comeback left
9. WR - streak left (40 yards)
10. HB - zig zag run (30 yards)

Additional Instructions: On all pass routes, make sure all breaks are the proper depth from the line of scrimmage. Realize that you will be running these routes to the right and to the left side of the formation. Also, on pass routes the caller will state the defender is man, inside, outside technique or zone and then you must make your route adjustments. The only time your spot on the field will change is when you go from an inside receiver to an outside receiver or vice versa.

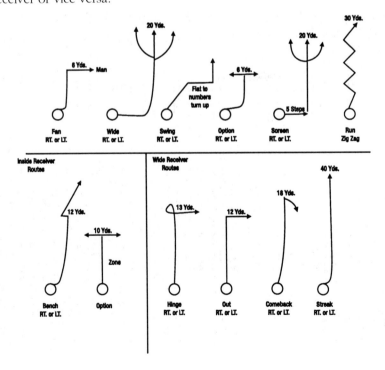

ABOUT THE AUTHOR

Tom Zupancic has been the strength and conditioning coach of the Indianapolis Colts for more than ten years. A graduate of Indiana Central University, he was a four-year grid letterman and a three time collegiate wrestling champion. Tom was part of four USA National Wrestling teams touring Europe. He reached the final Olympic trials in 1980 and 1984 in Greco-Roman Wrestling. Ranking 14th in the world among all-time super heavyweights with a 600-pound bench press (set in 1988), Tom won the WPF World Bench Press Championships in 1990 with a 600-pound lift and finished second in the Strongest Man in America contest in 1992.

Tom keeps busy away from the weight room with charitable and public appearances. Along with lifting demonstrations, he gives talks on goal setting and positive thinking.

SOME THOUGHTS ON *CONDITIONING FOR FOOTBALL ... AND THEN SOME* AND ITS AUTHOR TOM ZUPANCIC

In the thirty plus years I have been involved in the NFL, one area that has changed the most is the emphasis on strength and conditioning. Being involved in a solid off-season program gives a player a physical as well as a mental advantage that carries over to the football field. In today's NFL, players as well as coaches need an edge. Following the program Tom Zupancic has designed in this book will help provide that winning edge.

Ted Marchibroda
Head Coach, Indianapolis Colts

Zup has helped me train and rehabilitate from injury. I have also watched him help and motivate others. Experience and his hands-on approach are his greatest assets. He shares his methods of training and innovation in this book.

Will Wolford
All-Pro Tackle, Indianapolis Colts

Upon coming into the NFL, experts predicted that I wasn't going to make it. Through hard work and guidance from Tom Zupancic, I'm still standing better than ever in year number seven.

Jeff Herrod
Linebacker, Indianapolis Colts

Tom is a leader and innovator in the field of strength and conditioning. He is a master at linking a conditioning program with motivational skills to maximize each individual's potential for physical fitness.

George Catavolos
10-year professional
Defensive Back Coach